To

"Vida"

from

Nancy-Caroll Draper

THE GREAT DANE
Dogdom's Apollo

Am. & Can. Ch. Dinro's Diplomat, owned by Robert E. Heal.

In memory of Rosemarie Robert

Left to right: Ch. Dinro Aelric and Ch. Dinro Aslan,
owned by Rosemarie Robert.

Ch. Dinro Taboo Again, owned by
Rosemarie Robert.

THE GREAT DANE

Dogdom's Apollo

by

NANCY-CARROLL DRAPER

1981

First Edition—First Printing

HOWELL BOOK HOUSE

230 Park Avenue   New York, N.Y. 10169

Library of Congress Cataloging in Publication Data

Draper, Nancy-Carroll.
  The great dane.

  Bibliography: p. 202
  1. Great Danes. I. Title.
SF429.G7D7   636.7′3   81–6404
ISBN 0–87605–162–X   AACR2

Contents

About the Author

MISS DRAPER, owner of the well known Danelagh Kennels (reg.) in Ridgefield, Connecticut, has been successfully breeding and showing Great Danes for nearly 40 years.

Her family was among the earliest breeders of Irish Wolfhounds in America and also bred Labrador Retrievers and English Springer Spaniels.

Miss Draper has been an approved AKC judge for 12 years, during which time she has judged at every prestigious show in America including Westminster Kennel Club in New York, International Kennel Club in Chicago, Santa Barbara Kennel Club in California, Kansas City Kennel Club and Westchester Kennel Club in New York.

She has judged in Canada, England, Sweden, South Africa and Ireland.

As a member of the Great Dane Club of America since 1944, she has served on its Constitution and By-laws Committee, is currently Chairman of the Standard Committee and the Educational and Symposium Committee, and is a member of the Color Research Committee and Publicity Committee.

Her international associations include Honorary Member of the Great Dane Breeders Association (England), The Great Dane Club (England), the Scottish Great Dane Club, the Deutscher Doggen Club (Germany), the Swedish Great Dane Club, the Irish Great Dane Club, East African Wildlife Society, and a Vice-President of the South African Great Dane Association.

Miss Draper served in the Connecticut Legislature for four terms as a State Representative, at which time she was responsible for all dog legislation and was appointed to the Governor's Commission for the revision of all state canine laws.

A member of the Wyoming Stock Growers Association, Miss Draper raises Charolais cattle in Cody.

She is also closely connected with the Buffalo Bill Historical Association, which is comprised of The Whitney Gallery of Art, The Winchester Museum, The Plains Indian Museum and The Buffalo Bill Museum.

Her interest in the art and photography of animals has paralleled her practical experience in such matters, and her own collection of animals in sculpture and painting is considered outstanding.

Acknowledgments

No VOLUME of this kind can be successfully completed
without the help of many others who, in varying ways and means, give
of their time, wisdom and efforts. I offer my sincere gratitude here to
all those who have helped so much in the completion of this work.

A special vote of thanks to Mrs. Paddy Magnuson for her expertise in
the chapter on grooming and training; Mrs. Rose Sabetti for her chapter
on Obedience; the Buffalo Bill Historical Association for the rare pho-
tograph they kindly supplied; Mr. Donald Gauthier and the Great Dane
Club of America for the reproduction of the Illustrated Standard; Mr.
Al Feldman, past President of the Great Dane Club of America, for his
advice and assistance; and an extra thank you to all those many good
friends and acquaintances who were so kind in sending me so many
pictures to choose from for the book; however, for various reasons beyond our control—such as unavailability—some pictures were not forth-
coming.

My particular thanks to my friends Dr. J. E. Mosier of Kansas State
University for his two chapters and to Dr. Kenneth Doeg of the University
of Connecticut for his chapter. Also, a special thank you to Mrs. Freda
Lewis and Miss Jean Lanning of Great Britain for their help on the
American Great Dane in England, to Dr. Monica Stavenborn and Mrs.

Ingrid Skaar for the American influence in Sweden and to Mr. Kozo Kato and his interpreter, Dr. Joseph Morita, for their most valuable information on the state of the Great Dane in Japan.

To my secretary, Jeanette DeFazio, and to Karen Schemm, for their hours of practical and material help in the mechanics of putting together this manuscript and all the accompanying pictures, my heartfelt thanks.

Final Acknowledgment

Last, but far from least, I want to thank Jon Messman who, as a professional writer, has spent hours of his time assisting me with this book. Without his help, I doubt this effort would have come to fruition.

Nancy-Carroll Draper
Danelagh Kennels

Author's Note

NUMEROUS OTHER BOOKS have been written on the Great Dane. This volume, however, concentrates on the Dane in America and the influence of the American Dane on others. This work is written for the clear and concise understanding of the breed today.

For the first time there is a chart showing the major bloodlines and kennels over a span of forty years. The origins of these lines were, of course, in Germany or England. However, previous books on the breed have covered thoroughly that area of Dane history.

It has also been my interest to show the development of the Dane through a comparison with the early Standard to the present day Standard. The reason for the Color Code of Ethics is brought out in Dr. Doeg's chapter on genetics. The original colors are included from a very early German book to stress why we must maintain a Code of Breeding in the chapter on the Code of Ethics.

Rose Sabetti's discussion of Obedience is an important part of this volume. She was one of the first people in this country to organize an Obedience Club. The Dane in Obedience is a challenge for an owner, proving that one must also breed for brains.

Throughout, I have tried to keep in mind that there are few large kennels today and that the majority of Daneites live under different conditions from those of the '30s.

I hope the discussion on art with a mention of stamp collecting will stimulate an interest in these fields and present another dimension to the art of dog breeding.

N.C.D.

1

The Pages of Time...

THE WARM WIND of the sirocco blows across the blue Aegean. The man stands facing the water, his linen *chiton,* gathered over one shoulder, moving gently in the wind. He is a proud man, noble in spirit and action, a warrior of ancient Greece. His land is the land of intellect and emotion, of mind and body, beauty and strength. It is the land of Plato and Aristotle, Virgil and Homer, the cradle of Western Civilization. At his side stands a giant dog, truly an Apollo of dogs, a dog fit to match the warrior's pride and nobility. This great dog, specially bred in the district of Molossia in Epirus, is known to the warrior as a Molossian Hound. We know this dog today as a Great Dane.

At the gates of Nineveh in ancient Mesopotamia, an Assyrian huntsman is about to go into the fields. He moves easily in his close-fitting tunic with its twin cords of woollen tassels, his strong bow fashioned of eucalyptus wood. Moving with him are two huge, smooth-coated hounds who strain at heavy leather leashes, eager to fly across the red clay soil. To the huntsman, they are Assyrian Giant Hunting Dogs. Today, we call

11

them Great Danes.

The Roman Emperor, Vespasian, sits in the center of the great amphitheater he has built. We know it today as the Colosseum. The Romans called it the *Amphiteatrum Flavium.* Vespasian leads the assembled thousands in cheering the blood sport spectacle going on before him, giant dogs fighting with bears, bulls and even tigers imported for the events. Vespasian and all of ancient Rome knew these massive dogs as Giant Fighting Hounds. They are, to us, Great Danes.

Pre-biblical Assyria, Egypt, ancient Greece and the Roman Caesars all knew the dog which we today call the Great Dane. Moreover, and more importantly, they knew not some hardly-recognizable, far-removed version of the Great Dane but a dog which clearly and unmistakably is the forerunner of our modern Dane. On friezes and tablets, coins and carvings, the dogs pictured are entirely recognizable and entirely distinct from other large breeds present in those times, notably the Greyhound, Saluki and Mastiff hound.

The remarkableness of this fact is made more so when we consider the tremendous variety of breeds we have today. This is a purity of heritage which is the result of more than simple breeding practices. It bears upon another kind of purity which we must understand to properly comprehend the uniqueness of the Great Dane, the "King of Dogs."

This kind of purity can be called the genetic or evolutionary purity. There are less than a handful of dogs which possess such evolutionary purity, that direct line back to the origin of the *Canidae* as a family. Therefore, in order to properly understand and admire the breed as it is today in our modern Great Dane, it is necessary to understand something about the dog itself, the family *Canidae.* To do this, the usual history of the Great Dane must be viewed differently, divided into three segments rather than two commonly used. Ancient and modern history is not enough. Evolutionary history must be a part of any proper understanding of our breed.

This is because the evolutionary history of the Great Dane (and that of a precious few other breeds) is one with that of the *genus Canis.* In the development of the Danes we have today, we can trace how they have descended with an evolutionary purity from the original animals which became man's friend and ally in the dim mists of prehistoric time. Many writers, poets and sentimentalists, and indeed many naturalists, were fond of believing that ancient dog attached itself to man. Modern behavioral science, reconstructing what we know of the hunting patterns and capabilities of ancient man and the wild *Canids,* believe that the very opposite was true.

Early man was a lone hunter but it is not difficult to imagine how his primitive mind, observing the pack hunting methods of wild dogs, recognized the advantage of communal hunting. Primitive man, it is now believed, attached himself to wild dog packs in the hunt. As man developed primitive weapons, the reverse happened. It must be remembered that the *Canids* already possessed a social intelligence. The hunting pack is a basic example of social intelligence and this fitted them to recognize an alliance with man and his primitive weapons was a beneficial relationship. Such an alliance, or the recognition of it, would have been impossible were they also solitary hunters. In any event, that partnership began millions of years ago and has existed to this very day.

But man developed into the questing, thinking, highly-specialized organism he is today and the modern dog is an example of man's ability to channel genetic knowledge into specialized forms. With no other living thing—not with flowers, not with cattle, fish or plants—has man developed so many varieties of species as he has done with his "best friend." All one has to do is compare the Pekingese and the Greyhound, the Chihuahua and the St. Bernard, to be struck by the extent to which man has genetically engineered the dog.

But man's knowledge of genetics was not enough to make this possible. He was helped by the unique, evolutionary genetic heritage of the dog. The dog is what biologists term a physiologically *plastic* organism, meaning simply that the dog possesses a genetic adaptability to change through selective breeding. By contrast, the feline family, the cat, has also been subjected to man's insatiable need to experiment. Yet the results have been far different. The tiger and the house tabby are essentially different only in size and strength. The cat, regardless of its natural varieties and the domestic variations man had bred, is very much of one pattern. Efforts to develop a wide variety of cats have never achieved anywhere near the results of those with the dog. This is because the evolutionary heritage of the feline resulted in an organism relatively fixed or phylogenetically rigid.

The genetic plasticity of the dog can be traced back 40 million years, to the origin of the canine as a family. A creature called *Miacis* was the common ancestor of both bear and dog. From *Miacis* came two descendants, *Daephanus* and *Cynodictus,* the latter evolving into *Tomarctus,* the first direct ancestor of our modern dogs. *Daephanus,* a large, heavy-tailed animal, was the first of the bear-dogs and evolved into a larger and still heavier animal until he changed from the running habits of the *canids* to the lumbering gate and heavy skull, progenitor of our present-day bears. *Tomarctus* evolved into the wolves, foxes, jackals, hyena-dogs and wild dogs which are still with us today.

The modern genetic plasticity of dogs can be traced to this evolutionary plasticity and it is this hereditary history that has allowed man such wide results with his genetic experiments on the dog. It is this quality which has enabled man to breed giant dogs and tiny dogs, dogs with long hair and short hair, dogs designed for the heat and for the arctic, for hunting and for sitting around on pillows, dogs which hardly bear any resemblance to each other as a family.

But a few of our contemporary breeds have, in anatomical structure and in true *canid* instinct patterns, retained a remarkable degree of evolutionary purity. They have been refined but not changed. Of these few breeds, the Great Dane is one. While there is a great deal in the evolutionary period millions of years ago which is still unknown to us, we do know that the fossil remains of dogs have been discovered dating back to the Bronze Age. Excavations in Denmark have revealed prehistoric dogs with anatomical construction very close to that of modern dogs. From this anatomical evidence on hand, we can see a type of prehistoric dog which definitely excludes most of our modern breeds. The archeologist, Strobel, found remains of prehistoric dogs in Italy and these dogs were large, long-limbed, fleet, intelligent (based on size of cranial structure) and can reasonably be considered a Great-Dane type. It is clear, then, that the Great Dane possesses an evolutionary purity as well as the purity of bloodlines and breeding of modern practices.

Five thousand years ago

The ancient history of the Great Dane begins with a period some 3,000 years before Christ. On the tombs of the Egyptian ruler, Beni-Hassan, there are carvings of dogs which in size, comformation and appearance are certainly early Great Danes. In fact, one of these "tiger dogs" is clearly a form of harlequin. That these carvings are not depictions of Greyhounds, another of our oldest breeds, is evidenced by the presence in other wall carvings of a longer, lighter, Greyhound type dog.

The Egyptians revered the dog and it is interesting that the quality of loyalty we so value in our modern dogs also existed as part of the canine character in the days of ancient Egypt. The Egyptians considered the dog a symbol of fidelity. Every Egyptian city had its dog cemetery for canine mummies and when a dog died, the entire family went into a period of mourning.

From these cemeteries, we confirm that there were a number of different sizes and types of Egyptian dogs. Yet when picturing a dog on

14

their sacred places they always chose the dog we consider an early Dane, according this breed (and perhaps the Greyhound and Pharaoh Hound) that signal honor. In the Metropolitan Museum of Art in New York City, there is an Egyptian toy, a carving of a dog running, which could well be a figurine carved yesterday of one of our modern Danes with uncropped ears.

Greece

The early history of the Dane shows not only evidence of existence, but the fact that the Dane was consistently accorded a place of honor by various civilizations. In the Royal Museum in Munich there is a Grecian coin of the fifth century B.C. that shows a dog so closely resembling a Dane that no other reasonable assumption is possible. Over four centuries later the Dane still appears on the Greek Cunobeline coin of 39 B.C.

From archeological excavations, we again know that other canines existed in that era. Yet Greece, cradle of western civilization, chose the Dane to appear on its coins, its sculpture, its places of honor. Why? Because ancient Greece worshiped the unity of beauty and strength. They held these two elements as characteristics of their gods. They tried to emulate the unity of beauty and strength in their culture, their architecture, their sculpture, even in their athletics. It is little wonder, then, that the ancient Greeks found the Dane perfectly suited for depiction on their coins, the dog most thoroughly embodying these twin ideals. The Romans, who drank heavily at the wellspring of Greek culture, adopted these ideals as their own and continued to picture the Great Dane in numerous ways and places.

The Middle Ages

In medieval times, the Great Dane continued to be used for hunting and guarding throughout Europe and the British Isles. Medieval tapestries continue to depict the Dane in use, showing Saxons hunting the wild boar in English preserves before the Norman conquest with dogs of a definitely Great Dane type. Numerous writers and artists have depicted early Great Danes during these times but among the most prominent was a Frenchman, Gaston de Fois, who wrote an authoritative and still widely respected work in 1387, *Livre du Chasse* . . . the Book of the Hunt. De Fois had as many as 1,000 dogs in his kennels and when his book was later profusely illustrated, among the dogs were some called *Alaunts*, unques-

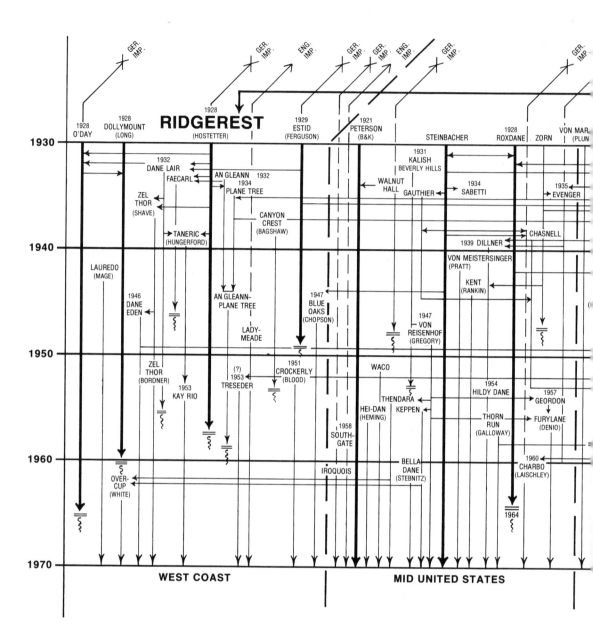

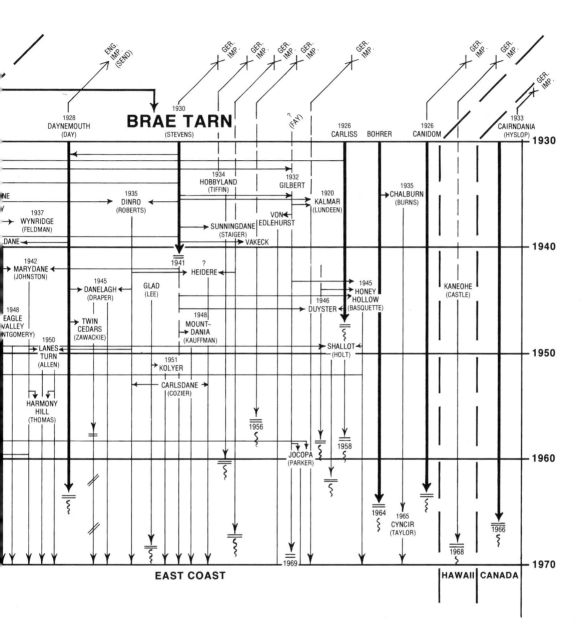

tionably Great Danes with heavy, square muzzles, cropped ears and true Dane body and size. In 1580, Antonius Tempesta of Florence, Italy, shows a Great Dane. Both men distinguished between these *Alaunts* and Mastiffs and Greyhounds.

In 1686 the English engraver, Richard Blome, shows a boar hunt in his work, Gentlemen's Recreation, with dogs unmistakably Great Danes, one a Harlequin. The Dane was very much present during the Renaissance period as witness the works of many Renaissance artists, notably Rubens and Veronese. In the 17th and 18th centuries, many writers, poets and artists made mention of the Great Dane, including Alexander Pope who wrote often of his own faithful Dane.

Whence the Name?

As concrete literary and visible artistic evidence exists of the evolutionary and historical purity of the Great Dane—a record in carvings, pictures and words of the continuity of the breed—the name continues to be steeped in mystery and obscurity. Outside of one reference in Edward's *Cynographia Brittanica* to the "Danish dogs," and Blome's boar hunt which takes place in Denmark, there is no evidence of a Danish role in the history of development of the breed. How, then, the name Great Dane?

The German Influence

Numerous theories have been put forth but the truth is that no one knows the answer. What we do know is that in late medieval years, as the population of Britain increased, the wolf and wild boar decreased. The English Danes almost vanished from the British Isles. The center of Dane breeding became middle Europe, particularly in Germany. The Germans certainly were the greatest adherents and fans of the Great Dane during the eighteenth and nineteenth centuries and can rightly claim credit for bringing us the Dane we now know. But even the Germans with their meticulous record-keeping and their middle-European preoccupation with correct nomenclature, had trouble naming their baronial guard dog.

At one time, the term German Boarhound was widely used because of the breed's activities in hunting the wild boar through German and European forests. In those days, the Dane was the hunting dog of the kings, barons and noblemen just as he once was for the Assyrian and Greek warriors. By night, he was guard and protector of the huge Rhineland estates. Old German steel and copper engravings afford ample proof that the "boarhound" was indeed the Dane. Then, later, various regions of Germany began using different names for the breed: *Ulmer Dogge; Tiger Dogge; Danish Dogge Hetzrüde* (Chase or Chasing Dog); *Metzgerhund* (Butcher Dog) and *Deutsche Dogge*. It should be noted here that the term *dogge* does not translate into our word *dog*. The German *dogge* means mastiff. The German for dog is *hund*. *Tiger*, in German, refers to white with dark patches, such as a pinto pony (*tigerpferd*) and obviously refers to a harlequin.

In any case, all this confusion of names was too much for the orderliness of the German mind and as all the regional appellations were names for the same breed, the German Government decreed in 1870 that the breed be properly and officially called *Deutsche Dogge* (German Mastiff) and made distinct thereby from the ordinary mastiff which they simply refer to as Mastiff. It is said that Bismarck, the Iron Chancellor, himself took a hand in the official designation for he was an avid fancier of the Dane and always had one or two at his side, even when holding court. Two of his favorites, Tyras and Sultan, were well known throughout all of Europe.

Today, in Germany, the breed is called *Deutsche Dogge*, in France *Dogue Allemand*, in Sweden *Grand Danois*, in Italy *Alano* and in America and England, Great Dane. But, as William Shakespeare observed, a rose by any other name would still smell as sweet. A Great Dane, regardless of the name, is still the Apollo of dogs, one of the very few evolutionary and historically pure breeds.

The modern history of the Great Dane can be traced to two countries which were paralleling each other in their upward mobility, intense vitality and nationalistic fervor. The first of these countries was Germany, the Germany victorious following the Franco-Prussian War, the Germany developing a nationalistic image for almost everything within its borders. This was the era of Bismarck, the Iron Chancellor, and the full flowering of the great Rhineland baronies. Castles overflowed with art and sculpture; the German royal courts echoed the overtures of the fanciest days of French royalty. The other country was that turbulent, rising giant, America, a land eager to adopt the very best of Europe, reaching out to draw in all it could swallow, be it people, architecture, manners or dogs.

The Dane Comes to America

Great Danes were imported to America in the middle eighteen hundreds. The famous Indian scout, Buffalo Bill, Colonel William Cody, had a Great Dane as a boy. The Dane, named Turk, was buried at the Cody family grounds in Wyoming. In 1857, Mr. Francis Butler owned a Dane said to measure 37 inches at the shoulder.

But upon first coming to America, the Great Dane almost developed even more nomenclature troubles. If you walked the streets of the old south or the midwest 75 to 100 years ago with a Great Dane at your side, you might well have heard the dog referred to as a bloodhound. In those days, the play *Uncle Tom's Cabin* by Harriet Beecher Stowe, had become one of the most popular offerings by traveling road show companies. The story itself is credited, on one level, with the raising of the American consciousness to the evils of the slave system and becoming a very potent political melodrama. On the purely theatrical level it provided a very effective stage vehicle. At one point in the play, Eliza is chased cross the ice by bloodhounds. But the bloodhounds proved to be very poor actors. They were so lethargic and doleful that they brought nothing to the chase. They ambled across the stage instead of running. Producers began substituting the early Great Danes in the country when they found that the Dane temperament allowed the dogs to quickly get into the spirit of things. The Danes could be excited to simulate a real chase across the stage.

However, they continued to refer to bloodhounds in the dialogue of the play and often in program notes and the original book, of course, told of blodhounds. It didn't take long for entire segments of the population in the south and the midwest to mistakenly take the Great Dane to be a bloodhound and we know how extensive use of any term, no matter how incorrect, can bring the term into general acceptance.

But with the end of the Civil War, the traveling road show companies of *Uncle Tom's Cabin* found other stories to perform and more Great Danes were appearing in America to rescue the proper name. But the Dane had narrowly missed another example of nomenclature problems on this side of the Atlantic.

The German dogs continued to be imported into this country through the early 1900s, but then the American breeders began to play an ever-increasing role in the development of the Great Dane we know today. Though German breeders continued to produce dogs and supply top foundation stock to American breeders, the first American breeders can rightfully take credit for eliminating the strong strain of unbridled viciousness which the breed once possessed and later for eliminating much of the coarseness in the early Danes. With the best of German bloodlines imported here, and with the fine work of early American fanciers, the Great Dane developed into the dog embodying those twin ideals of the ancient Greeks . . . beauty and strength, inseparable and intertwined.

20

The great American Dog "Prince."

2

The Great Dane in America

THE FIRST KNOWN RECORD of any Great Dane in the United States of America was in 1857 when Mr. Francis Butler brought a harlequin named Prince from New York to London. Whence Prince came, no one seems to know. He was shown in London and the *Illustrated News* carried a drawing of Prince and his master. Indeed, there was such interest in the big dog that Mr. Butler was received by Queen Victoria.

Great Danes were not shown in America under their present name until the late 19th century, however. In 1877 there were eleven Great Danes entered in the Philadelphia Grand National Show under the name of "Siberian" or "Ulm" dogs. In 1878, the Westminster Kennel Club had a class of Great Danes under the same name of "Siberian" dogs. Again, there were eleven entries.

Possibly the first major show in which the Dane appeared as Great Danes was in 1881 at the American Institute Building in New York. It was a fashion-conscious crowd at the show, women in the latest silks and the fashionable *polonaise* gowns, men wearing the newest style imported from Monte Carlo, the dinner jacket. The well-dressed crowds turned in awe as owners and handlers appeared with the striking, imposing huge dogs called Great Danes. They crowded around the ring, eager to see and watch these impressive and magnificent animals being shown. However, it was a major debut both auspicious and inauspicious. The Danes were so bad-tempered and started so many fights during the show, amongst each other and with every other breed, that they were barred from further show competition. Not for seven years, in 1888, were they shown again in an American ring.

But the Great Danes shown that day in 1881 were of direct stock if not actual dogs out of the great castles of the Rhine where the dogs were maintained as hunting companions by day and guard dogs by night. They exhibited a ferocity found only in trained attack dogs which, in many instances, they were. The vast German royal estates demanded guard dogs of size and aggressiveness. It is a tribute, indeed, to those early American Dane breeders that in less than twenty years they were able to reduce that facet of the Dane character and virtually eliminate the unmanageable bad temper. The Danes shown in 1890 were well behaved and safe to handle. It is a further tribute to the selective breeding of those original American Dane fanciers that the Dane's original protectiveness traits are still present in our modern Danes but now surrounded by balanced temperament.

As the breed became better known in America, fanciers continued to look to Germany for good specimens and breeding stock. The "Deutsche Dogge" had been recognized in Germany for twenty years and strong measures had been instituted there to protect breeding stock and to regulate breeding standards, color codes, etc. The result was that many excellent, sound dogs were being produced.

The Founding of the Great Dane Club of America

In 1884, C.H. Mantler began raising Great Danes in the United States and his interest and love for the breed undoubtedly had a strong influence on furthering the development of the breed in this country. Mr. Mantler "exhibited" his first Dane in 1895. On May 3rd, 1889, he was one of 33 persons who established the "German Mastiff" Club in Chicago, Illinois and that same year it became the fourth breed club to join the American Kennel Club, making it certainly one of the oldest of all breed clubs. In 1891, the German Mastiff Club became the Great Dane Club of America, at which time it was transferred to New York City and eventually incorporated under the laws of New York State.

At about the same time another set of fanciers in New York formed another club devoted to the breed. This, the United States Great Dane Club, had as its first President Mr. William DeForrest Manice. Its officers and board of directors were gentlemen of the banking, brokerage and merchandising world. Eventually, this organization gave way to the present Great Dane Club of America but it is of value to note that there was indeed an active, early fancy interested in developing these giant dogs in America. The first President of the Great Dane Club of America was Mr. A. H. Heppner. In 1892, the first Great Dane Club of America trophy was offered at the Westminster Kennel Club Show. It was won by a dog named Ch. Melac owned by Mr. Herbert G. Nichols of Chicago.

A dog named Wenzel won over Melac later that year but it was generally conceded that the most superior Dane of the year came out of Indiana, Major McKinley. In 1898, Charles E. Tilford imported the magnificent Sandor von Inn. A rich, dark brindle, Sandor could win a championship against today's Danes. Shown against the finest of homebreds and the very best of German imports, he was never beaten during his active show career.

In 1897, Mr. Mantler, a well-known breeder and judge by then, accepted the post of Secretary of the Great Dane Club of America, a position he held until 1922. He was then elected President and served in that capacity until 1938. The famous Mantler trophy was only recently discontinued.

In 1898, the first official by-laws of the Great Dane Club of America were accepted by the American Kennel Club. Also, the first official standard of the Great Dane was adopted. The popularity of the breed had increased so much by that year that Westminster had an entry of 29 puppies, 35 dogs and 15 bitches. The judge, J. Blackburn Miller, Vice President of the Club, awarded the breed to the German import Sandor von Inn.

Early Leading American Breeders

The history of the Great Dane in America would not be complete without mentioning some of the early outstanding breeders and the dogs they imported. The East and California were the major centers with many German imports going to both coasts. The present-day kennels all owe their backgrounds to the oldtimers of the breed who were: C. Ludwig in the early 1900's, Peterson 1921, Kalmar (Lundeen) 1920's, Carliss 1926, Canidom (Kapp) 1926, Daynemouth (Day) 1928, Roxdane (Ehmling) 1928, Bohrer approximately 1928, J. Steinbacher approximately 1928, Estid (Ferguson) 1929, Cairndania (Hyslop) 1930, Brae Tarn (Ste-

24

Am. & Can. Ch. Reichsiegerin Senta Hexengold, German import owned by Mrs. Betty Hyslop.

Am. & Can. Ch. Senta Hexengold and friend, owned by Mrs. Hyslop.

vens) 1930, Gilbert 1932, and Warrendane (Warren) 1935.

Some of the dogs imported by Mr. Stevens were Ch. Quia von Loheland, Ch. Czardas von Eppeleinsprung-Noris, Ch. Lionne v. Loheland, Ch. Tiger Hexengold, Ch. Nero Hexengold, Ch. Randolf Hexengold and Ch. Reh von Loheland of Brae Tarn. Mrs. Hostetter imported Ch. Etfa v. d. Saalburg, Ch. Irmin v. Odenwald, Ch. Remes v. d. Rheinschanze. Col. Ferguson imported Ch. Ozelot v. Birkenhof, Ch. Zelia v. Loheland, and Ch. Oerlang v. Loheland. Meanwhile, Dr. Spengard imported Ch. Cyrus v. d. Pissa and Ch. Reise v. Loheland, later owned by Laura O'Day. The Warrens imported Ch. Nanda v. Loheland, Ch. Jamas v. Loheland, Ch. Wirbelwind v. Loheland, Ch. Blitz v. Schloss Staufeneck of Warrendane. Betty Hyslop, a long-time Canadian breeder who showed extensively in the United States, contributed a great deal to the breed history in this country and was an early member of the parent club. Mrs. Hyslop imported Ch. Aslan v. Loheland, Ch. Inge Hassia, Ch. Senta v. Hexengold, Ch. Quagga v. Loheland and Ch. Pax v. Birkenhof.

The midwest also acquired its new additions to the breed. The Harkness Edwards of Walnut Hall Kennels in the early 1930's imported Ishulan v. Loheland, Ch. Fionne and Ch. Ferguni v. Loheland, and International Ch. Gunnar v. Hollergarten. The Kecklers of Vakeck Kennels in the late 1930's brought into Ohio Ch. Wasdan v. Loheland of Vakeck.

From these dogs came the next generation of top kennels: Beverly Hills (Kallish) 1931, Kaneohe (Castle), and Faecarl (Dr. and Mrs. McPheeters) early 1930's, Zel Thor (Shave) early 1930's, Planetree (Hawkins and Martin) 1934, Hobbyland (Tiffin) 1934, Chalburn (Burns) 1935, Evenger 1935, Dinro (Robert) 1935, Canyon Crest (Bagshaw) middle 1930's, Gauthier in the middle 1930's, Murray (Maude Murray), Taneric (Hungerford) late 1930's, Chasnell (Williams) late 1930's, Wynridge (Feldman) 1937 and Rose Sabetti, 1934.

In the 1940's came Ladymeade (Jewel), moved from Great Britain in the middle forties, An Gleann-Planetree (McKeeby) in the middle 1940's, Twin Cedars, (Zawacki) middle 1940's, Marydane (Johnston) 1944, Honey Hollow (Basquette) 1945, Danelagh (Draper) 1945, Duyster 1946, Dane Eden (McEdwards) 1946, Blue Oaks (Chopson) 1947, Von Riesenhof (Gregory) 1947, Alldane (Jensen) 1948, Mountdania (Kauffman) 1948, Eagle Valley (Montgomery) 1948. Also in the forties were Hy Crest (Sawyer), Shallott (Holt), Foray (Litchfield), Jotunheim (Buse), Laurado (Mage), Anadane (Pierce), Von Meistersinger (Pratt), Kent (Rankin), Heidere, Knajar (Knapp), Geritom (Kelly) and Matchett.

And so down to the beginnings of the modern-day Danes—Lanes Turn (Allen), Turkadana (Baskind), Crockerly (Blood), Fury Lane (Denio), Hildydane (Dillner and Compton), Geordon, Hei-Dan (Heming), Iro-

26

Ch. Faecarl's Brendo, owned by Dollymount Kennels, Tacoma, Wash.

Ch. Dane Eden's Samson

27

Am. & Can. Ch. Inge Stussia, German import owned by Mrs. Hyslop.

Buffalo Bill, his mother and sisters. Turk on left.

quois (Andrews), Kay-Rio (Kenosita), Keppen, Kolyer, Charbo (Laishley), Thendara (Larsen) Jacopa (Parker), Bella Dane (Stebnitz), Harmony Hill (Thomas), Treseder, Von Overcup (White), Carlsdane (Cozier), Temple Dell (Temple), Cyncir (Taylor).

Following these dogs and breeders of the 1950's came a newer generation of Dane breeders leading up to and including today's fanciers dedicated to carrying forward the great heritage in their hands—Lincoln, Riverwood Ranch (Robinson), Magnus (Magnuson), Davis, Umpachene (Farquharson), Regene (Horne), Ozark Crest (Sundstrom), Radcliff, Broadway (Morris), Starlight (Lipschultz), Larica (Riccio), Brookdane (Guerin), Tallbrook (White and Twaits), Tivoli (Bleeker), Von Reseac (Mitchell), Meyer's Dane (Meyer), Sunridge (Lawrence), Haltmeier, Edeldane (Thompson) Locust Hill (Brown), Bluspru (Glanz), Pinehurst (Huseby), Sheenwater (Chandler), Hay-ron (Rahn), Crestwood (Miller), Four Winds (Carren), Strawser, Dane Oaks (Joinnides), Rojan (Cataldi-Cochran), Wallach, Nahallac (Callahan), Tamerlane (Morey), Lovett, Sounda (Bone-Layne), Harris, Norella (Jackson), Devrok (Ecker), and so many, many more which space just does not permit us to list. They will carry on and be joined by still others in the decades to come.

Footnote to Americana

It is amazing that, in reading all the books on the Great Dane, and exploring the many anecdotes and tales of Danes and their famous masters, no American has heretofore mentioned Colonel William Cody, the famous "Buffalo Bill." Perhaps the fact that I have seen the paintings in the Buffalo Bill Historical Association and the Whitney Gallery of Art in Wyoming had something to do with uncovering the fact that Buffalo Bill did own more than one Great Dane. According to the book, *Last of the Great Scouts*, by his sister, Helen Cody Wetmore, a black Great Dane, Turk, was Will Cody's constant companion. In his own words, Buffalo Bill referred to Turk as an "Ulm dog," as well as "tiger-mastiff," "German Mastiff," boarhound and Great Dane. When the family moved from Iowa farther west, it was Turk who spotted the game and gave chase as well as providing constant watchfulness to warn of intruders to their camp or on the trail. When finally settled in the new territory designated under the Kansas-Nebraska Bill of 1854, it was Turk who was appointed to look after the five children. One day he saved Bill's sisters from attack by a panther by pulling them into a shallow hole he dug for them. He covered the girls with leaves and as the panther attacked, so did Turk. He was dazed and bleeding, but wounded as he was, he had returned to the fight to try to save his charges when suddenly Bill arrived and shot the mountain lion. Luckily, Turk was not critically wounded and Bill's joy and love for his dog were deeply expressed.

The anecdote of Turk saving Bill's father one night from a murderous drunken ruffian is most amusing. Father was ill upstairs when a man came to the house to kill him. Mother and Bill fed him plenty of whiskey trying to deter him, but on leaving, the man stole Bill's pony. Bill sent Turk after him. Turk nipped the man's heels which were practically on the ground due to the size of the pony. Finally, on a signal from Bill, the pony threw the villain and Turk stood over him until Bill called him off.

Shortly thereafter Bill's father died and Bill started taking odd jobs to provide for his mother and the other children, leaving the faithful Turk to be a companion and a guard at home. One day just after Bill had returned from a trapping expedition, a rabid dog appeared and bit Turk. When they realized what would have to be done, the hired man was called to shoot Turk but was not allowed to use any of Bill's guns. A sad funeral procession by the entire family took place, and somewhere on Cody Hill there is still a red bloodstone carved with the name "Turk" upon it. The following poem is quoted from the book:

THE BURIAL OF TURK

Only a dog! but the tears fall fast
    As we lay him to rest underneath the green sod,
Where bountiful nature, the sweet summer through,
    Will deck him with daisies and bright goldenrod.

The loving thought of a boyish heart
    Marks the old dog's grave with a bloodstone red;
The name, carved in letters rough and rude,
    Keeps his memory green, though his life be sped.

For the daring young hero of wood and plain,
    Like all who are generous, strong, and brave,
Has a heart that is loyal and kind and true,
    And shames not to weep o'er his old friend's grave.

Only a dog, do you say? but I deem
    A dog who with faithfulness fills his trust,
More worthy than many a man to be given
    A tribute of love, when but ashes and dust.

Even though Buffalo Bill had lost his beloved Turk, in other pictures of him in later life touring Europe with his Wild West Show, there is seen another Dane, this time a fawn or brindle.

30

Ch. Lillian's Mr. President, owned by Kenneth O. Peterson.

Meyer's Dane Tu-Mŭch, owned by Mrs. Fred Meyer, Jr.

31

Left to right: Am. & Can. Ch. Vi-Daynes Arpege of Sandy Knob, Ch. Charbo's Silver-Bel of Vi-Bayne and Vi-Baynes Samatha. Littermates, photo taken at nine months.

Ch. Lane Turn's Gunnar, owned by Mrs. Leo Allen.

3

The American Dane Overseas

THE INFLUENCE of American Danes in England, Sweden and Japan gives a good indication of the increasing impact American-bred dogs and American bloodlines have had throughout both hemispheres. Because of the original preeminence of German breeders since the turn of the century, and the geographic location of Germany itself, it was only natural that German Danes exerted a great influence on all Dane breeding in the European and Scandinavian areas for many years. However, since the end of World War II, and especially in the past decade, American dogs and their bloodlines have begun to have a major influence on the international breeding scene.

German, Dutch, English and French dogs are still a major element in Danes in the countries discussed here but more and more foreign breeders are actively seeking the qualities of the American Dane today. It is not an exaggeration to say that American Danes and their bloodlines have become prized acquisitions on the international scene. The examples given here of the American Dane in England, Scandinavia and Japan reflect the work of the American Dane breeders in producing desirable

Eng. Ch. Fergus of Clausentum, breeder-owner Jean Lanning.

Eng. Ch. Walkmyll Jaegar, breeder-owner Mrs. Freda Lewis.

34

and spectacular Danes. Space permits us to list only those American kennels and breeders which have exerted the major influence internationally during the past few decades. We are certain that there will be many others, both old and new to Danes, who will carry on the influence of the American Dane in other lands. But only the continued soundness, and the scrupulous attention to the stable breeding practices, will maintain the excellence of American Danes as both a goal for ourselves and an example for foreign breeders.

American Danes to England

In England, where the English have been breeding Danes since at least the 15th century, they have developed their own style of Dane. From the early 1900's, German stock was imported to England and vigorously used by English breeders. But in 1967, the noted English breeder and judge, Jean Lanning, visited America and was immediately impressed by the very high level of quality of our best Danes. She purchased a dog from Danelagh Kennels, which was named Danelagh's Quillan of Clausentum. Quillan came out of a half-brother and sister mating to Ch. Dinro's Taboo. Miss Lanning wanted just such a tightly-bred dog for her kennels and Danelagh's Quillan of Clausentum became the first modern American Dane to profoundly influence the English dogs. He sired the spectacular Ch. Fergus of Clausentum who produced nine champions of his own. Fergus won under Australian, American, Swedish and Swiss as well as English judges.

The Danelagh line also became the American basis for the Walkmyll Kennels' many champions in England, producing for them Ch. Walkmyll Kaster of Clausentum, Ch. Walkmyll Storm, Ch. Walkmyll Duncan, Irish Ch. Walkmyll Claudius, Ch. Dorneywood Dahlia of Walkmyll and Ch. Halemoss Bettina of Walkmyll. In 1976, Freda and Ron Lewis of Walkmyll Kennels imported to the shores of Britain Danelagh's Eurus of Walkmyll whose grandmother on the dam's side was Quillan's sister. They also imported Danelagh's Eloise of Magnus. These dogs are now making their American heritage felt in English show rings.

Hazel Gregory's Von Reinsenhof Canis Major, out of Dinro's Taboo, was introduced into Jean Lanning's Kennels.

The American Influence in Sweden

Sweden has been forward-reaching in the importation of American

Great Danes. Ulla and Curt Magnussen in their Airways Kennels, have been especially active in bringing the American Dane to their country. In 1956 they imported Duyster's Euclid of Ralwin, "Candy," who became International and Nordic champion. The following year they purchased Candy's mother, Swedish Ch. Duyster's Joan of Arc. Bred to Ch. Faust v. Washburn, she produced two champions. When, in 1962, they bought Int. and Nordic Ch. Airway's Dinro Beau Geste, a dog out of Ch. Dinro Taboo and Thendara Megaera, he became a top winning dog in Scandinavia and produced 20 champions, one of whom, Int. Ch. Colorado, was the top winning dog in Sweden. They then imported Danelagh's Kaisa who became Swedish champion.

In the mid 1960's, the Magnussens obtained two Harmony Hill dogs, Linda and Lied. Both earned International and Nordic championships and in 1969, Linda was the top-winning dog of all breeds in Sweden. Lied produced 34 champions, a record never before equaled in any breed in Sweden.

In those same mid-sixties, the lovely harlequin bitch, Dinro's Lucky Charm came to Sweden and produced harlequin Swedish champions. The fawn bitch, Flaming Pride of Hazeldane also made her presence felt in Sweden, a daughter of Ch. Danelagh's Jason. In 1972, Harmony Hill again entered the Swedish Dane scene with Harmony Hill Fjord's Fancy (Swedish ch.) and Harmony Hill Fjord of Airways (Int. and Nordic ch.). Both dogs began producing outstanding progeny at once.

Ingrid Skaar imported Danelagh's Alfhilde from the United States which went on to become International and Nordic champion. She then imported Paddy Magnuson's Mayo of Magnus who was bred in Sweden to Danelagh's Alfhilde and went on to become a Nordic champion.

The major American bloodlines affecting Swedish Danes over these decades have been Duysters, Dinro, Danelagh and Harmony Hill.

The Impact of American Danes in Japan

The history of American influence on Danes in Japan is a relatively recent one but that influence has made up in impact what it lacks in longevity. Until 1973, only German Great Danes had been imported into Japan, except for an occasional outsider of no measurable influence. This was primarily due to the fact that a Mr. Katsura, who headed the Great Dane Society of Japan, a man of prestige and influence, strongly favored the German Dane. According to the eminent breeder and owner of Sunnyside Kennels in Japan, Mr. Kozo Kato, only a very few people who subscribed to the German Dane journals also subscribed to the American

Dynasty Star Border, owned by Kozo Kato.

Sunnyside's Happy Hobe, owned by Kozo Kato.

magazines, *Dane Dispatch* and *Great Dane International.* Only this small group was aware of the differences in American and German Danes and of the tremendous advances in the American Dane quality.

Of those few, Mr. Kato was one and he had been perhaps the greatest advocate of the American Dane for Japanese breeding programs. When he first brought American Danes back to Japan, his advocacy was demonstrated in immediate, visual terms and a fast-growing core of Japanese fanciers immediately joined his enthusiasm. The structure of the Dane world in Japan is one which causes inherent problems to the conscientious breeder and is certainly very different than it is here. The dog community of Japan is made up of two major clubs, the Japan Kennel Club (JKC) and the Kennel Club of Japan (KCJ). Dane fanciers, as those of any breed, can belong to either or both clubs. In addition, there is an independent Dane organization called the Great Dane Society of Japan. All three organizations sponsor dog shows under their own judging policies and winning systems, which vary from one to the other.

Membership in the Great Dane Society of Japan consists chiefly of German Great Dane adherents. KCJ members are mostly breeders, many of whom now favor the American Dane and are studying extensively the techniques and problems of breeding good dogs. The majority of the JKC members are pet-shop owners. It is quickly obvious that special problems must arise from this situation. The future of the Great Dane in Japan is therefore even more dependent on the integrity and the breeding practices as well as the philosophy of the individual breeder operating in a climate which is, if nothing else, something less than co-ordinated.

Nonetheless, in less than a decade, the impact of American Danes and American bloodlines has been astonishing. At the major dog shows held in Tokyo and Osaka recently, it was hard to find a purely German Great Dane while American Danes and their progeny were most conspicuous. Mr. Kozo Kato's advocacy of the American Dane has been a major factor in this emergence. His strict breeding programs and his attention to good breeding practices have also played an important role in the changing Japanese Dane picture and in this he has been joined by other Japanese fanciers. They have also come to American shores to obtain the kind of stock they want to see in the Great Dane in Japan. These are, primarily, Mr. Tsuruya, Mr. Camo, Mr. Natori and Mr. Sakayori, fanciers who are most anxious to improve the Japanese Dane.

Mr. Kato has stated to us that American Danes bred to German Danes in Japan have not produced favorable results. Japanese breeders have had far happier success breeding American males to American females they have imported for just this purpose. Mr. Kato began his import

38

program mainly with the Dinro line before Rosemarie Robert's tragic death in 1978, with the Dinro dogs and Mrs. Robert's breeding program still intact. He imported Dinro DeWolf's Jason who became perhaps the major stud of his program and produced a number of Japanese champions. Mr. Kato also imported for his Sunnyside Kennels, studs and bitches from Kolyer Kennels, Kolyer's Rion and Kolyer's Tara-Tsa as well as others and dogs from Sheenwater Kennels. From the west coast, he imported several fine harlequins from Riverwood Kennels.

Mr. Tsuruya imported dogs primarily from Jecamo Kennels and the Van Neff Kennels; Mr. Camo from Von Riesenhof Kennels, Mr. Natori from Ozark Crest Kennels and Mr. Sakayori from Riverwood Kennels in California.

The kennels that have exerted the major influence on Japanese Danes in less than a decade are, then, Dinro, Kolyer, Jecamo, Riverwood, Von Riesenhof as well as the other names mentioned above. It will be a matter of future fascination to see which new kennels and breeders will continue to carry the banner of the American Dane overseas—for one thing is almost certain, American Great Danes and the results of their bloodlines, will be in ever-increasing demand so long as we maintain the quality and excellence present breeders have achieved.

Dane character.

4

Great Dane Character

THE MODERN GREAT DANE reflects the efforts of Dane breeders and the basic, innate aspects of thousands of years of genetic purity as a member of the canine genus. The Dane, therefore, is a dog of multi-faceted character. A Dane can be gentle. A Dane can be rough. He can be playful. He can be quiet. He can be noisy. He can be sweet. He can be fierce. One must live with Great Danes to fully appreciate the many sides of their personalities.

But it is this very many-sidedness which accords the Dane what is possibly the greatest single quality he possesses, that of adaptability. A Dane can adapt to the ways and personalities of a wide variety of people, a trait not found in many breeds. Raised from puppyhood, a Dane will adapt to the climate, habits and life styles of its owners. A Dane will be active with active owners or sedentary with inactive ones, gentle for gentle owners and aggressive with militant families.

The Dane is intelligent in the real sense of that word. At one time the great body of scientific thought held that intelligence was learned, acquired through education, experience or observation. This capability to acquire knowledge and to retain what has been learned is the kind of intelligence the usual IQ tests endeavor to measure. It was considered that everything else was pure instinct, not related to intelligence at all.

More and more, science has come to recognize the element called instinctive or intuitive behavior as a definite kind of intelligence, very different from empirical knowledge or the intelligence of experience, yet an equally valid kind of intelligence. It defies precise measurement and in many ways is still an unknown element. We know what it does but seldom why or how. We also know now that both mankind and animals possess it in varying amounts. Instinctive intelligence is what permits a dog to be afraid of fire without the actual experience of being burned. It is what enables a dog to be aware of many subtle forms of danger without visible or tangible evidence of that danger. It is a quality which not all individual dogs nor all breeds possess in equal quantities.

Those who know the Dane agree on the breed's high level of instinctive intelligence. A Dane usually senses when it is time to be quiet, to be cautious, and when it is time for steady watchfulness. A Dane observes when it is time for observing, plays when it is time for playing and barks when barking is in order. In short, a Dane senses the meaning and spirit of the moment and this takes more than simple canine instinct. It takes instinctive intelligence.

The inevitable question arises: how is the Dane with children? A Dane properly brought up with and around children is invariably excellent with youngsters. The Dane character is one of understanding and will take a great deal more from children than most of the snappy breeds. But let us be truthful. Few dogs of any breed do well with children unless they are raised with or in the company of children and learn the ways of children.

The Dane character is like the physical stature of the Dane—drawn in large strokes. There is nothing small, snappish or petty about the Dane character. The traits we have come to expect of dogs in general—faithfulness, companionship, love, protection—are all kingsized in the Dane. Because of his great size and strength, the Dane is not for every owner and every household. A Dane made ill-tempered by poor surroundings and improper handling can be really dangerous. Unlike some of the more lethargic, large breeds, the Dane reacts quickly and because of his flexibility reflects the atmosphere of his surroundings.

There is one additional side to the Dane character, the side most prized by those who know and love the breed. This quality can be rightly termed constancy. The mature and developed Great Dane is almost always constant in nature. If the dog has been raised to be friendly and gentle, it will be just that. If the Dane has been raised as a playful companion, it will be that. Conversely, if he has been raised in a tense, aggressive atmosphere, he will be that. But the important thing is that the constancy will remain. This enables the owner to know what his or her dog will do and won't do in a given situation, unlike the temperamental uncertainty found in some breeds. The owner can know how his Dane will act with children, with men, with women, with postmen, with large strangers and small ones, those with loud voices and those with soft ones. The Dane will be constant in all these things in almost all instances. Those who have experienced the unpredictability of some breeds know how comforting this constancy can be.

It is perhaps most accurate to sum up the Dane character with the words of Lord Byron: ". . . all the Virtues of man, without his Vices."

Ch. Murlo Caesar of Stonehouse, owned by Murray & Lois Michaels.

Am. & Mex. Ch. Jecamo's Beefeaters Marcus and friend, owned by Jecamo Kennels.

5

Choosing a Puppy

Stop, Look and Think

Before you buy a Great Dane puppy, before you buy *any* puppy, stop and look at yourself, your family, your own likes and dislikes. Certain breeds have certain characteristics, physical and emotional attributes that are part of their individuality as a breed. You wouldn't wear a dress or a suit that wasn't right for you. You wouldn't choose a car that didn't fit in with your family and its needs. Yet many people buy a dog without giving any real thought to what they need, to what fits their temperament and their life style. This is always a mistake. When you buy a dog you are adding a new member to your family, a new dimension to your life. Be sure it is the right addition for you. Pick the right breed for yourself and your home. Take a good, long look at yourself and your likes, at your temperament and disposition. High-strung, quick-moving people are never happy with placid, slow-moving dogs. A sedentary person is never really at ease with a bundle-of-energy breed. Once you are fairly certain a breed is the right one for you, you have overcome half the problems.

The Great Dane, fortunately, has a variety of innate characteristics which can be brought out, a pliable temperament which can be developed to fit your desires. But the Great Dane is not the dog for everyone nor for every home. Given the right owner, it is the most rewarding of companions, the most magnificent addition to your home.

Once having decided that a Great Dane is the right dog for you, the next step is choosing a healthy, happy one that will grow into the dog you want it to be.

Picking a Puppy

Where you buy your puppy is important, very important, but there are certain things you should look for wherever you buy it. A healthy puppy should have the following: *eyes* clear and bright; *ears* free of odor, cropped and clean inside; *nose* clean, free of discharge; *gums* pink and firm; *coat* clean not scaly nor dry; *bones* large and well-covered; *personality* friendly, playful, unafraid.

Be certain your puppy is registered, or is eligible for registration, with the American Kennel Club and that you receive a color-marked certified pedigree. Obtain a record of your puppy's worming, temporary inoculations and a record of any permanent inoculations for distemper, hepatitis and leptospirosis.

Examine your puppy to be certain that, if a male, he is not a monorchid. There are only five acceptable Dane colors: fawn, brindle, black, blue and harlequin, a black-and-white parti-color dog. Anything else is unacceptable.

If possible, see the immediate parents of your puppy. When grown, he may exhibit many of the same physical and emotional traits. The breeding of any living creature is a matter of knowledge and the combinations of hereditary matching, which are infinite. There is no guarantee of anything in dog breeding, only the reasonable projections of experienced and honest breeders. A champion sire or dam is of meaning, indicating a certain level of quality, but even a champion must be bred to the right mate for the desired results. So the honesty, reliability and knowledge of the breeder is of utmost importance.

Where and Why

Would you shop for a quality item in a bargain basement? Would you expect to buy something outstanding from a pushcart vendor? Of course, you wouldn't. And, of course, people have gotten rare bargains, lucky finds, doing just that. But those are the exceptions, not the rule.

Because your Great Dane is not an ordinary dog, not in size nor in power, not in his ancestry nor his temperament, not in his very essence, it is even more important that he be bought from the right place, which is his breeder who knows his dog, knows background, heritage, individual family characteristics and a host of other things. Now what about breeders? Aren't there a great number of them? Yes, there are. There are famous names, old-line, highly reputable breeders with large kennels and there are breeders with only a few dogs. The important thing is that your dog comes from a kennel and breeder who adheres to the ethics, code and standards of the Great Dane Club of America.

A reputable breeder adhering to that code of ethics is not a middle man interested only in traffic in dogs, in buying and selling and nothing more. A good breeder is interested in selling the right dog to the right people, the right dog for the right home. His reputation depends on that. His business depends on that. But most of all, his concern for his dogs governs that.

So we say it is very important where you buy your Great Dane. A list of breeders and kennels, large and small, may be obtained from the American Kennel Club or the Great Dane Club of America. An even more fun way of finding a breeder and a dog is to go to dog shows, just as you go to any other exhibit or showroom before making an important purchase. At a show you can watch, study, meet people, learn and have fun doing it.

A Grown-up in the House

Sometimes, the raising of a puppy Great Dane poses particular problems. A word for the purchase of a mature dog should be considered. Most breeders do not have mature dogs for sale as pets but sometimes they do have and if the dog comes from a reputable kennel there are many sound reasons for the purchase of a grown dog, one over a year old. Such a dog eliminates many problems which, to certain people, may cause undue difficulties. A grown dog is invariably leash-trained and house-broken. Careful care of growing legs and feet, early training, etc., are all past. A grown dog is instant protection and there is no conjecture as to how he or she will turn out.

Using just plain common sense will make rubbish out of the reasons commonly heard against acquiring the grown dog. Give him time to get used to you and you to him. He has developed his personality, likes and dislikes. These can be altered, given time, but they must be taken into account meanwhile. Great Danes are highly adaptable dogs. Given respect, common sense and time, a new grown-up in the house can be an ideal addition.

Bed and Board

You have purchased your puppy and you want him home, naturally. Different breeders recommend varying ages for bringing home your puppy. This is a personal decision dependent on various factors, the individual puppy, your own home, etc., but the cropping of the ears is usually done between six to eight weeks. Your breeder will give you proper instructions on the care and future taping of the cropped ears. You should also receive detailed instructions on feeding, inoculations, diet supplements, etc.. Find a veterinary, preferably one experienced with Great Danes, and have your puppy looked over, just for everyone's peace of mind.

Great Dane puppies grow very rapidly but their bones are nonetheless puppy bones. Do not overtax your puppy's strength by too much playing or exercise, particularly jumping. Great Danes, because of their weight, are quick to develop unsightly callouses on their elbows unless they have soft bedding to lie on. This is important to your dog and should be provided as soon as the puppy is brought home. Exercise is a balance of the right kind at the right time and the right amount. This will depend on the individual dog and your breeder should be consulted with any questions in this regard.

Recipe for Happiness

Take your Great Dane, feed him correctly, give a dash of diet supplement, a large measure of proper discipline, good surroundings and plenty of grooming, mix well with lots of love and you will have a companion of beauty, loyalty and love, an extraordinary addition to your home. Where else can you find that kind of return for your efforts? No place. We don't think so, anyway.

6

Training, Grooming
and Ear Taping

IF YOU HAVE ACQUIRED a young show prospect, training
should begin immediately so that you can establish a happy relationship
with the puppy and his environment.

The early training can be accomplished without the puppy even being
aware that he is being molded for the big time.

Handle the puppy frequently, play with him, and every now and then
set him up in a show stance using the command "stand-stay." He will
probably move his feet just as soon as you get them placed, but make a
game of it and patience and perseverance will win out. Praise and reward
all his efforts.

Teach him to stand-stay for his daily grooming. He may roll over on
his back a few times, but again patience and consistency are your role.

Puppies quickly learn to enjoy the daily brushing, toweling and the
extra attention. Grooming time is also a good time to work in some of
the show ring procedures such as examining teeth, eyes, testicles, setting

up, baiting, etc. However, never force an issue and gradually the puppy will gain confidence and trust.

Teach him to gait with his head up at an easy pace by your left side, on a loose leash, neither lagging or pulling. He must learn to gait in a straight line and in a circle—counterclockwise.

If there are training classes available or puppy matches in your area, by all means attend these functions. This exposes the puppy to other dogs, crowds, and an atmosphere he cannot get at home.

Come show time you will want to present your puppy properly groomed as well as properly trained, and while a Dane's short coat makes it a fairly simple procedure, it is amazing just how much effect a little clipping and cleansing can have.

Nails should be trimmed back as short as possible a few days before the show. This may be done with nail clippers, hand file or electric file, or combination of clippers and file. If you do use nail clippers and accidentally cut too close to the quick, it may bleed profusely. Don't panic. If you do not have a styptic stick handy, powdered alum, sugar or even just a tissue pressed on the offended nail for a couple of minutes will generally stop the flow.

Ears should be cleaned with a piece of soft cotton, dampened in alcohol. Q-tips are not to be recommended for this procedure as the inner ear is very sensitive and easily damaged, and they could be injurious if they dig in too far or if the puppy shakes his head unexpectedly.

The hair along the edge and on the inside of the ear should be trimmed with scissors, regular razor or electric razor. The electric razor does the neatest job, but you will have to accustom the puppy to it gradually. A piece of cotton temporarily placed in the ear will dull the sound of the razor while the hair is being removed.

On a dog that will positively not permit scissoring or a razor near his ears, one of the human hair removal ointments such as "Neet" may be used successfully. If this is resorted to, it should be tested first to insure there is no allergy present.

After razoring or scissoring, a little cod liver oil ointment soothes the skin.

Eyes should be checked for any discharge and may be wiped clean with a tissue. On a hot windy day, dust can sometimes set up an irritation and cause "red-eye." Vizine is useful in such cases, or a solution of boric acid powder and water is equally good.

Now the coat—many puppies hang on to their puppy coat an extraordinarily long time until they look like a woolly, spotty mess.

There are many kinds and varieties of grooming tools on the market nowadays, from the regular old dandy brush, to gloves with metal spikes, quick-shed blades, etc.

Some success in removing dead hair has been claimed by the administration of mineral oil to the coat, then grooming with a rubber curry comb or rubber glove. This method seems to work on older dogs, but is not so effective in removing puppy coat.

The quick-shed blade can be quite effective, but should be used cautiously, as Danes have very sensitive skin, and you could draw blood on the blade as well as hair.

The regular daily coat grooming should show satisfactory results if one uses either a rubber curry comb or rubber glove, grooming first with the grain of the coat, then against the grain, and then smoothing back down by grooming with the grain again. This should be followed by a good rub down with a towel, or even with your hands.

On show day, many use a coat spray to get a little extra shine to the coat, but this is not recommended for daily use as some sprays make the coat sticky, and some attract insects such as bees.

Fawns, brindles, blues and blacks that are groomed regularly seldom need bathing before a show. But the harlequin can be something else again!

That is not to say that harlequins do not keep themselves as clean as the other colors. They do most of the time—until the day before a show—then watch out! Wintertime they find the mud, and summer time rolling in the tall grass is a delight. Apart from these hazards, bathing is really the only way to insure that the white is at it's "whitest" when a harlequin enters the ring.

When one does have to resort to bathing, it makes it a lot easier if the dog will get into the bathtub.

Soak the coat thoroughly, then use either a baby shampoo or regular dog shampoo, and rub gently through the coat, leaving the head to the last. Rinse thoroughly, preferably with a spray to be sure you get all the shampoo out of the coat.

On a warm summer day the dog can be rubbed down with a big bath towel and then allowed to finish drying in the sun. Avoid drafts. If you do dry him outside, be sure to keep him on a leash and in control, otherwise the first thing he will do is roll in the grass or whatever, and void all your efforts.

Now for the final touches. Whiskers should be scissored off the muzzle, under the chin and over the eyes. The hair along the flank and along the back of the hind legs should be trimmed.

A final inspection and rub down with a clean towel just prior to going into the ring will complete the picture of a clean, well cared for exhibit.

50

Ear Taping

This is such an important part of the grooming and cosmetic aspects of Dane care that I have thought it best to discuss it apart from all the other elements in good care techniques. Proper ears are a vital part of the esthetic appearance of your Dane. No one knew this better, and understood the problems more fully, than the late Rosemarie Robert of the Dinro Kennels. Therefore, I can think of no source more authoritative from which to quote and to borrow on this subject and I shall make use of the countless conversations I have had with her and of the numerous articles she has written on the subject in addition to the lectures she often held regarding this vital part of Dane care.

Too many novices still believe that the cropping is the all-important element in good ears. Of course good cropping is important and this requires someone who can evaluate the head on your puppy and do an ear that will fit the head. But as in medicine, the best surgery can be destroyed by poor postoperative care. This postoperative care is, for our Danes, the business of proper ear taping. The entire object of cropping an ear is to make it stand up beautifully. It is the taping, the aftercare, which must accomplish that, not the cropping itself.

When to crop? This should not always be a matter of age though usually the puppies will be between six to eight weeks at the right time. However, Rosemarie Robert always used an additional, more personal (for the dog) gauge of when to crop, measuring from the knob inside the puppy's ears to the tip of the ear—4¼ inches for males and 4 inches for females. This takes into accurate account the fact that not all puppies grow at the same rate.

When the ears have completely healed, the proper taping can be done in the proper way. In this technique, you should abide by five rules. Indeed they are a credo of proper ear taping:

    1—Always tape a clean, dry ear.

    2—Always clean the inside as well as the outside.

    3—Never tape over an unhealed edge.

    4—Never tape in a hurry; be slow and careful.

    5—Be sure the ear is standing straight and tall when you've finished.

Now, for the particulars. Rosemarie Robert favored the use of corset stays, ¼ inch wide. These may still be obtained at many sewing centers or from old girdles. If they are not available, it is important that you hunt about for any plastic piece of the same general width, pliability and consistency. Next, a cork, preferably from a thermos bottle, a wide cork of approximately 1¾ inches in width; some corks from large magnum wine bottles will fit these measurements. Lastly, waterproof adhesive tape in

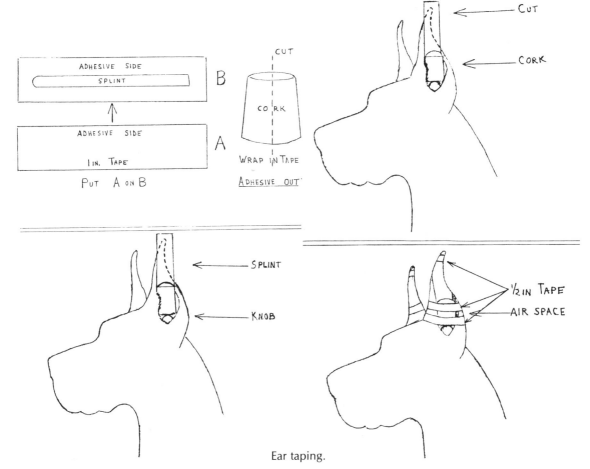

ADHESIVE SIDE	**B**
SPLINT	
↑	
ADHESIVE SIDE	**A**
1 IN. TAPE	

PUT A ON B

CUT

CORK

WRAP IN TAPE

ADHESIVE OUT

CUT

CORK

SPLINT

KNOB

½ IN TAPE

AIR SPACE

Ear taping.

1 inch width.

These are your basic tools. A note of caution against the use of wooden splints such as tongue depressors in place of the pliable corset stays. Puppies at play tend to break the stiff wooden splints and the entire taping must be done again if this happens. You want a splint that has give to it.

Clean the interiors and exteriors of the ears thoroughly with rubbing alcohol. Again, using the knob inside the puppy's ears, measure the length of the ear from knob to tip, then cut your stay to fit. Place the cut stay on the *adhesive* side of your 1 inch tape. Cut the tape at the ends but be sure to leave ¼ inch at both ends of the splint. Cut another length of tape to the same size as your first one. Lay this second piece of tape over the splint now on the first piece of tape with the *adhesive side up.* (See accompanying diagram 1 as drawn by Rosemarie Robert.) Your splint will now be between the two pieces of tape but only one adhesive side of the tape will be outward. This is the side you will press to the inside of the ear.

Cut the cork in half now (see diagram) and take one half of it and wrap it completely in the adhesive tape, with the *adhesive side out.* Use other half of cork for other ear, wrapping the same way. You now have your corks and stays ready for use. Cut the 1 inch tape lengthwise to make it ½ inch (or get ½ inch tape and use). Cut the ½ inch tape in two strips, one about 14 inches long, the other about 2 inches long. These will be wrapped around the ears.

Place your adhesive wrapped stay against the inner part of the ear so that the one end fits against the cup on the knob at the bottom of the ear (see diagram). Center the upper end of the splint against the tip of the ear. Now take your adhesive wrapped cork and put it against the stay (splint) with the *flat side out* (see diagram.)

The next step, wrapping, is where many people err in the taping process. Taking the 14 inch length of adhesive strip, first wrap the bottom of the ear where the cork is against the stay to secure it. In wrapping the tape, be sure to leave the back part of the ear with at least a half-inch of space not covered by adhesive (see diagram.) When this is not done properly, when an airspace is not left, and the ear is completely wrapped with the adhesive, the ear "sweats" and causes infection to set in. This is a vitally important point in the taping.

When you've wrapped the cork and secured it in place, which in turn is holding the stay, take the 2 inch strip and tape it around the top of the ear (see diagram.) Note: leave a little air-space at the tip of the ear. This is also important.

Now you've taped both ears. Cut another ½ inch wide strip of adhesive about 12 inches long. Use this to tie the two ears together as reinforcement. Tie this bridge at the bottom of the ears, not the top which is another error often made (see photo.) Strengthen the bridge of tape with a few turns of extra tape where it joins the ears.

Taping should last until the ears start to outgrow the splint, usually in 4 to 6 weeks. If the stays are bent in play, bend them back again. Of course, if they are really broken, the ears must be retaped but the importance of the pliant stays with give in them is just to prevent the need for retaping. Check the ears constantly for any sign of split edges or infection which may come from rough play. The procedure for retaping the larger, longer ears is exactly the same as outlined herein. The need for proper measuring and airspace does not decrease at all. Proper taping will give you the kind of ears your Dane should have and which are, in America, an integral part of your Dane's appearance.

Newly cropped puppy.

54

Ch. Dinro Simon Templar, owned by Dana Knowlton.

Ch. Nahallac's Niila v Nottingham, CD and son, Ch. Nahallac's Bogart, CD, owned by Mrs. Karla Callahan.

7

The Creature Comforts: Bedding—Housing— Kenneling

THE GREAT DANE is not an ordinary dog in any way and cannot be treated in an ordinary manner if you are to raise and keep your Dane healthy and happy. Large dogs have problems of housing and kenneling which smaller breeds simply do not. Size, weight and yes, strength, create a far different set of care-factors whether you plan to make your Dane a house dog or a kennel dog. There are, however, certain rules which are applicable to both house and kennel care. Because few owners in today's world entertain the prospect of maintaining a large, thoroughly professional kennel of fifteen mature dogs or more, I shall confine these suggestions to those who will maintain a house dog (or house dogs) and/or a small kennel facility essentially separate from their own living quarters.

The matter of sleeping conditions, first. Bedding is a most important factor in the care and condition of the Dane. House dogs should have their own mattresses, preferably with washable covers. Of course, the mattress can be a proper bed. No Dane, especially puppies, should be left to walk about or lie down on hard surfaces such as stone or concrete. The ideal is non-skid carpeting. Asphalt tile, rubberized tile or thick linoleum, any flooring which has resiliency in it, is infinitely better than concrete. Hardwood, uncarpeted, is not recommended for growing Danes. Even the rubberized tile flooring can be quite hard and for young Danes some sort of covering is recommended in addition to the covered bedding itself.

Great Danes, because of weight, are highly subject to sores developing on the elbows, hips and even the hocks. These sores most always are the result of lying down on hard surfaces. A study showed that a dog, any dog, will rise and lie down approximately five times during an hour, averaged over a twenty-four hour period. During the normal waking and watching hours, the dog may rise and lie down a lot more than five times an hour. During night sleeping periods, it has been found that a dog will rise and change position at least three times an hour. A casual observation of your own pet will bear these figures out.

This means that your Dane will come down on those gangly, growing elbows and legs one hundred and twenty times during a twenty-four hour period, for one reason or another. That fact provides its own case for the need of soft bedding for the growing Dane. It must also be remembered that the Dane does not have the thick, heavy protective coat around the elbows of some other breeds such as setters, Huskies and St. Bernards.

If you are keeping your Danes in a kennel situation, a bed constructed of wood to stand at least four inches off the flooring is a must. This bed must be covered with a soft material. Soft rugs which can be changed frequently, cut to size, are excellent. Covered foam-rubber pillowing or mattresses are excellent, but attention must be paid to the propensity of puppies to chew, gnaw and generally tear at things. Even a young Dane's jaw power is formidable and can quickly destroy outer covering of foam rubber products. We do not recommend wood shavings. Dogs tend to ingest them and unless changed frequently, they create a special kind of dust which is unhealthy for dog and owner to inhale. Newspapers are not soft enough and today's newspapers are printed with such high speed the ink is seldom dry and comes off quickly to make your dogs, your house and you dirty.

If you are kenneling your dogs, even a small kennel facility should be constructed so that ventilation is ample, especially during the hot weather. Heat travels upward in any enclosed space and will gather and press downward to become impossibly oppressive unless there is upper ventilation for it to escape. This also allows for the entrance of cooler air at a lower level to circulate. The services of a professional builder should be obtained if you intend constructing a wood or cinder-block structure. Always select a site that is not too far from your living quarters to reach easily in bad weather. A builder can provide you with most of the considerations you will need to construct a proper building but only a few builders are educated in kennel work. You might ask for a double floor with wire mesh or tar paper between the floors. This will create a warmer (in winter) kennel and a more draft proof structure. It will also protect against rodents, from field-mice to chipmunks.

Your kennel structure should ideally have attached outside runs. For Danes, these should be a minimum of twenty-five feet long and six feet wide. Fifty feet or more is ideal. Professionals should be consulted regarding the proper wire fencing but suffice to say that for Danes it must be heavy gauge and sunk firmly into the ground either deeply enough or into concrete strips. Danes can dig very large and deep exits for themselves.

Should your entire kennel facility consist of part-time outdoor runs, to which you bring the dogs in the daylight hours and return them to the house at night, investigate the various canvas and tarpaulin-type coverings which can be placed over the top of the runs. Even if your runs are part of a permanent kennel structure, these canvas tops can be very helpful in hot weather to shield the dogs from the direct sun. They come in attractive colors nowadays and often can be installed so they can be rolled entirely or partly back as you wish to cover only part of the run.

The flooring for outdoor runs is still often a matter of controversy. Concrete certainly is the easiest to clean and maintain, requiring only a frequent hosing-down. It is also hardest for germs to infect and breed in. However, it is also hardest on the legs and feet of dogs such as Danes. In winter, it tends to become icy and impossible for the dogs to maintain a footing and in summer it becomes a burning surface trapping heat. Medium to fine gravel is the best compromise for the surface of outdoor runs. It will not turn into mud under severe rain as ordinary soil will do, and it will provide better footing under ice conditions. It can be cleaned and, if expense permits, a metal or concrete drain along one edge of the runs can help in cleaning and ordinary drainage. Gravel can be disinfected to eliminate or control worms or other bacteria by a saturate salt solution or by use of a blowtorch. In extreme cases, it can be entirely replaced at a fraction of the cost of replacing an asphalt run.

Should your kennel structure be a permanent one, you will need to decide on the type of access and egress doors between the inner kennel and the individual outdoor runs. The manually operated individual overhead doors which can be opened and closed from outside the kennel enclosures are still the most favored. They must be properly fitted however to insure the least amount of draft in winter. Some kennels have had success with the type of free-swinging plastic door, usually made of lexan or some other form of fairly stiff plastic. These doors make it unnecessary for you to constantly play doorman and allow the dog to go in and out from kennel to run and back again at will. They close after the dog leaves one area for the other.

They serve as a great convenience to the kennel owner. However, they also limit your ability to confine the dog to indoor or outdoor areas. In winter, they do not furnish the draft protection of a closed, fitted door of substantial thickness. Some people have found the ideal solution is to use both kinds of doors, the overhead, manually operated ones in conjunction with the self-entry plastic kind. This allows you the convenience of the self-entry doors plus the advantages of closing the manually operated ones when you wish to do so.

If economics permit, a proper kennel structure should have a whelping room, individually heated, at one end of the kennel and a quarantine room removed from the main part of the kennel at the other end. Ideally, a quarantine area should be entirely separated from the kennel.

If you have a bitch and plan to breed her, a whelping box is definitely part of your bedding and housing needs. Ideally, a whelping box should be twice as deep and wide as the bitch is long and squared off on all sides. Provide soft bedding, topped by loose cloths which the bitch may paw into her own arrangements to satisfy the nesting urge. On three sides, the edges should be high enough to hold back drafts and keep in the puppies. The fourth side should be lower to accommodate easy access. Ideally, all four sides should have movable sides, or movable guard rails to permit you to increase the height of the sides as the puppies grow.

Even more ideally, your whelping box should have wooden slats or rails built outwards from the *inside* of the side walls. These will provide a haven for puppies, preventing the bitch from crushing them against the sides of the box. This is particularly helpful for large, heavy dogs such as Danes in the first few weeks of the puppies' lives.

Bedding should be changed regularly in the whelping box and the bitch should be allowed to sleep in the room with the box, and in it, for two weeks before the puppies are due. During the whelping itself, a piece of canvas, such as a painter's tarpaulin, can be put down over the bedding and simply discarded when everything is done and over with. Such a proper whelping box is necessary for your bitch whether it be placed in a kennel area or inside your house.

Ch. Abner Lowell Davis, owned by Mr. & Mrs. Lowell Davis.

60

Am. & Can. Ch. Heidere's Kolyer Kimbayh owned by Dr. and Mrs. James A Gribbin.

Ch. Archibald Davis, owned by Mr. & Mrs. Lowell Davis.

61

GROUP 1ST

WESTBURY
KENNEL CLUB, INC.
SEPT. 26, 1976

Ch. Cherokee of Dane Oaks, owned by Mr. & Mrs. Arthur Joinnides.

Ch. V Raseac's Great Caesar's Quote, owned by Gene Mitchell.

Am. & Can. Ch. Lincoln's Preilison, owned
by Mr. & Mrs. Craig O. McCaw.

Any kennel structure should contain a working fire extinguisher and a sand pail. A kennel used for commercial purposes must carry these items by law in many states. Some shade trees are nice to have near your kennel, especially the outdoor runs. But do not rush to construct your runs adjoining thick, close bush and tree growth which gathers in every sort of insect pest. Kennel runs should be surrounded primarily by free air.

If your kennel is air conditioned, the temperature during summer should be kept at about 75° and it is good practice to turn off the air conditioning for a half-hour before the Danes are let out to avoid the shock to the system of going from cool, dehumidified air into torrid, sultry air. Remember, a Dane's coat does not permit it to stand too much heat or too much cold. If your kennel is not structured for air conditioning, circulating fans can help a great deal to keep hot summer air cooled and moving. Such fans, but *not* fixed ones which blow the air in one direction, can also be used effectively around outdoor runs in the summer.

A final word about housing. Young Danes are very curious about everything, as are most all puppies, but Danes grow taller and stronger more quickly than most breeds. Enticing objects should be kept behind cabinet doors or high enough to be out of reach. This goes particularly for plastic objects, cups, umbrellas, children's toys, model airplanes and toy soldiers, some women's footgear. An object which one of the small breeds could gnaw on all day and only scratch the surface can be chewed into bits by a young Dane and swallowed with incalculable internal damage. A Dane bitch as a house dog offers seasonal problems which needn't cause panic. There are light plastic sheets sold all over for use as professional painters use drop cloths. These can be simply placed over your carpets for a few weeks, easily wiped clean and kept in place in a variety of ways.

Always remember, good housing and good bedding are as important for your Dane as they are for you.

Ch. Dinro's Neshobe Chief, owned by Miss Rae Beardsley.

Ch. Pandera of Carlsdane, owned by Hugh D. Cozier.

65

8

Standards

T HERE IS NO TOPIC more widely discussed, misinterpreted, misquoted, criticized, ignored among Dane owners, than the Great Dane Standard! Anyone professing a desire to become more than the owner of a pet Great Dane, be it an exhibitor, breeder, handler, judge or member of a Great Dane Club, should read *The Official Illustrated Great Dane Standard.* Study it. Memorize it. Forget other published visualizations, forget other written interpretations. Refer only to the Official Standard. After studying the Standard, ask yourself this question, "Do I like the Great Dane as it is represented in the Official Standard?" If the answer is not YES, change breeds . . . not the Standard. If you feel that the Standard should be changed to agree better with what you own, produce or are planning to produce, then you had better look over your breeding program and change it. You should be breeding to the Standard and not vice versa. The serious breeder, exhibitor and judge should read the Standard frequently. They must agree with it and follow its specifications or they should not be breeding, exhibiting or judging. It is the final and only authority on our breed. You selected the Great Dane for your breed;

Ch. Sheela's Scherazade, owned by Mr. & Mrs. James Blood.

Am. & Can. Ch. Danelagh's Zari, owned by Mrs. Paddy Magnuson.

in doing so, you also adopted the Standard. The Official Standard clearly describes the perfect Great Dane and this is what we should be breeding toward, this is what we should be exhibiting, and this is what the judges should be putting up at the shows.

The Standard is an attempt to picture the ideal specimen—it is not perfect—but it is the best possible guideline we have to breed toward and to judge by. People differ slightly in interpreting it, which is human nature. It is really specific in its definitions—e.g., mouth, top line, proper front, etc.—as well as color.

The main body of the Standard is what is important to learn—the *positive things* about our breed, not the tabulation of faults on the back page that makes one think negatively.

The Great Dane Standard is by far the most detailed and complete in dogdom—it is not out of date. Our Standard still follows the German Standard. Recent deviations in color covered under the Standard and the A.K.C. rule in Chapter 16 Section 9 strengthen it further.

We are aware that some fanciers are suggesting we make changes in the Standard—but if it is read and studied the questions being raised are already covered in it.

Therefore, let us get together for the benefit of the breed and breed according to our Standard.

We would suggest that all our local clubs conduct several programs on the subject of the Standard with their members whether in a panel discussion using illustrations, or with actual dogs. Our feeling is that today we have so many newcomers to our breed that it is here the clubs could perform one of their best services to our breed—education.

As a comparison with the revised Standard for Great Danes as approved by the American Kennel Club on August 10, 1976, we present an early Standard published in 1902.

The Early American Standard

STANDARD AND INTERPRETATION

(1) General Appearance.—The Great Dane should be remarkable in size and very muscular, strongly though elegantly built; the head and neck should be carried high, and the tail in line with the back, or slightly upwards, but not curled over the hindquarters. Elegance of outline and grace of form are most essential to a Dane; size is absolutely necessary; but there must be that alertness of expression and briskness of movement without which the Dane character is lost. He should have a look of dash and daring, of being ready to go anywhere and do anything.

Ch. Big Kim of Bella Dane, co-owned by Kay Stebnitz & Mabel Sheppard.

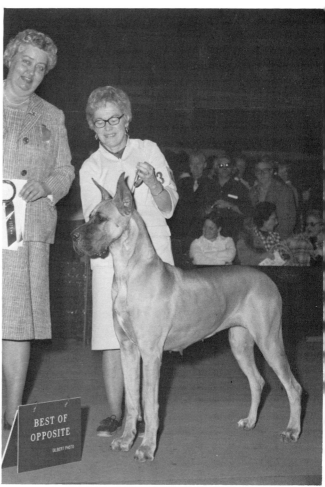

Ch. Mountdania's Heather, owned by Anna Mary Kaufman.

(2) Height.—The minimum height of an adult dog over 18 months old should be 30 in.; that of a bitch, 28 in.

(3) Weight.—The minimum weight of an adult dog over 18 months should be 120 lbs.; that of a bitch, 100 lbs.

(4) Head.—Taken altogether, the head should give the idea of great length and strength of jaw. The muzzle, or foreface, is broad and the skull proportionately narrow, so that the whole head when viewed from above and in front has the appearance of equal breadth throughout.

The entire length of head varies with the height of the dog; 13 in. from the tip of the nose to the back of the occiput is a good measurement for a dog of 32 in. at the shoulder. The length from the end of the nose to the point between the eyes should be about equal, or preferably of greater length than from this point to to the back of the occiput.

The skull should be flat, the occipital peak not prominent. There should be a decided rise or brow over the eyes, but no abrupt stop between them; the face should be well chiselled, well filled in below the eyes; the foreface long, of equal depth throughout. The cheeks should show as little lumpiness as possible compatible with strength.

(a) Lips.—The lips should hang quite square in front, forming a right angle with the upper line of foreface.

(b) Underline.—The underline of the head, viewed in profile, should run almost in a straight line from the corner of the lip to the corner of the jawbone, allowing for the fold of the lip, but with no loose skin to hang down.

(c) Jaw.—The teeth should be level and not project one way or the other.

Nose, Black and Brown a Fault

(d) Nose and Nostrils.—The bridge of the nose should be very wide, with a slight ridge where the cartilage joins the bone. (This is quite a characteristic of the breed.) The nostrils should be large, wide, and open, giving a blunt look to the nose. A butterfly or flesh-colored nose is permissible in harlequins.

(e) Ears.—The ears in natural state should set high on the skull and be carried erect, and cropped where this is permitted.

(f) Eyes.—Not too large and rounded, always dark, a brown or hazel color excepting in harlequins where any color and even different colors in each eye are permitted.

(5) Neck.—The Neck should be long, well arched, and quite clean and free from loose skin, held well up, snakelike in carriage, well set in the shoulders, and the junction of head and neck well defined.

(6) Shoulders.—The shoulders should be muscular, but not loaded; well sloped back with the elbows well under the body.

(7) Forelegs and Feet.—The forelegs should be perfectly straight, with big bone. The feet should be cat-like, the toes well arched and closed, the nails strong and curved.

(8) Body.—The body should be very deep, with ribs well sprung and body well drawn up.

(9) Back and Loins.—The back and loins should be strong, the latter slightly arched.

(10) Tail.—The tail should be thick at the root, and taper towards the end, reaching to or just below the hocks. It should be carried, when the dog is in action, in a straight line level with the back, slightly curved towards the end, but in no case should it curl or be carried over the back.

(11) Hindquarters.—The hindquarters and thighs should be extremely muscular, giving the idea of great strength and galloping power; the second thigh long and well developed, the stifle and hock well bent, the latter set low turning neither in nor out.

(12) Coat.—The hair should be short, dense, and sleek-looking; in no case inclining to roughness.

(13) Movement.—The action should be lithe, springy, and free. The hocks move freely, and the head carried high except when galloping.

(14) Color.—(a) Brindles.—Brindles must be striped. Ground color from the lightest yellow to deep orange, and the stripes must always be black.

(b) Fawns.—The color varies from lightest buff to deepest orange; darker shadings on the muzzle and ears and around the eyes are by no means objectionable.

(c) Blues.—The color varies from light grey to deepest slate.

(d) Blacks.

In all above colors white is only admissible on the chest and feet, but is not desirable even there. The nose is always black (except in blues, when blue is allowed). Eyes and nails preferably dark.

(e) Harlequins.—Ground color, pure white, with irregular black patches, having the appearance of being torn. Occasional grey spots not to weigh too heavily in judging. In this variety wall eyes, pink noses, or butterfly noses are not a fault.

Revised Standard For Great Danes

The Board of Directors of the American Kennel Club has approved the following revised standard for Great Danes as submitted by the Great Dane Club of America.

1. GENERAL CONFORMATION

(a) General Appearance.—The Great Dane combines in its distinguished appearance dignity, strength and elegance with great size and a powerful, well-formed, smoothly muscled body. He is one of the giant breeds, but is unique in that his general conformation must be so well balanced that he never appears clumsy and is always a unit—the Apollo of dogs. He must be spirited and courageous—never timid. He is friendly and dependable. This physical and mental combination is the characteristic which gives the Great Dane the majesty possessed by no other breed. It is particularly true of this breed that there is an impression of great masculinity in dogs as compared to an impression of femininity in bitches. The male should appear more massive throughout than the bitch, with larger frame and heavier bone. In the ratio between length and height, the Great Dane should appear as square as possible. In bitches, a somewhat longer body is permissible. **Faults**—Lack of unity; timidity; bitchy dogs; poor musculature; poor bone development; out of condition, rickets; doggy bitches.

(b) Color and Markings

(i) Brindle Danes. Base color ranging from light golden yellow to deep golden yellow always brindled with strong black cross stripes; deep-black mask preferred. Black may or may not appear on the eyes, ears and tail tip. The more intensive the base color and the more distinct the brindling, the more attractive will be the color. Small white marks at the chest and toes are not desirable. **Faults**—Brindle with too dark a base color; silver-blue and grayish-blue base color; dull (faded) brindlings; white tail tip. Black fronted, dirty colored brindles are not desirable.

(ii) Fawn Danes. Light golden yellow to deep golden yellow color with a deep black mask. Black may or may not appear on the eyes, ears, and tail tip. The deep golden yellow color must always be given the preference. Small white spots at the chest and toes are not desirable. **Faults**—Yellowish-gray, bluish-yellow, grayish-blue, dirty yellow color (drab color), lack of black mask. Black fronted, dirty colored fawns are not desirable.

(iii) Blue Danes. The color must be a pure steel blue, as far as possible without any tinge of yellow, black or mouse gray. Small white marks at the chest and toes are not desirable.
Faults—Any deviation from a pure steel-blue coloration.

(iv) Black Dane. Glossy Black. **Faults**—Yellow-black, brown-black or blue-black. White markings, such as stripes on the chest, speckled chest and markings on the paws are permitted but not desirable.

(v) Harlequin Danes. Base color: pure white with black torn patches irregularly and well distributed over the entire body; pure white neck preferred. The black patches should never be large enough to give the appearance of a blanket nor so small as to give a stippled or dappled effect. (Eligible, but less desirable, are a few small gray spots; also pointings where instead of a pure white base with black spots, there is a white base with single black hairs showing through which tend to give a salt and pepper or dirty effect.) **Faults**—White base color with a few large spots; bluish-gray pointed background.

(c) Size.—The male should not be less than 30 inches at the shoulders, but it is preferable that he be 32 inches or more, providing he is well proportioned to his height. The female should not be less than 28 inches at the shoulders, but it is preferable that she be 30 inches or more, providing she is well proportioned to her height.

(d) Condition of Coat.—The coat should be very short and thick, smooth, and glossy. **Faults**—Excessively long hair (stand-off coat); dull hair (indicating malnutrition, worms and negligent care).

(e) Substance.—Substance is that sufficiency of bone and muscle which rounds out a balance with the frame. **Faults**—Lightweight whippety Danes; coarse, ungainly proportioned Danes—always there should be balance.

2. MOVEMENT

(a) Gait.—Long, easy, springy stride with no tossing or rolling of body. The back line should move smoothly, parallel to the ground, with minimum rise and fall. The gait of the Great Dane should denote strength and power showing good driving action in the hindquarters and good reach in front. As speed increases, there is a natural tendency for the legs to converge toward the center line of balance beneath the body and there should be no twisting in or out at the joints. **Faults**—Interference or crossing; twisting joints; short steps; stilted steps; the rear quarters should not pitch; the forelegs should not have a hackney gait. When moving rapidly, the Great Dane should not pace for the reason that it causes excessive side-to-side rolling of the body and thus reduces endurance.

(b) Rear End (Croup, Legs, Paws).—The croup must be full, slightly drooping and must continue imperceptibly to the tail root. **Faults**—A croup which is too straight; a croup which slopes downward too steeply; and too narrow a croup.

Hind legs, the first thighs (from hip joint to knee) are broad and muscular. The second thighs (from knee to hock joint) are strong and long. Seen from the side, the angulation of the first thigh with the body, of the second thigh with the first thigh, and the pastern root with the second thigh should be very moderate, neither too straight nor too exaggerated. Seen from the rear, the hock joints appear to be perfectly straight, turned neither towards the inside nor towards the outside. **Faults**—Hind legs: Soft flabby, poorly muscled thighs; cowhocks which are the result of the hock joint turning inward and the hock

73

and rear paws turning outward; barrel legs, the result of the hock joints being too far apart; steep rear. As seen from the side, a steep rear is the result of the angles of the rear legs forming almost a straight line; overangulation is the result of exaggerated angles between the first and second thighs and the hocks and is very conducive to weakness. The rear legs should never be too long in proportion to the front legs.

Paws.—Round and turned neither toward the inside nor toward the outside. Toes short, highly arched and well closed. Nails short, strong and as dark as possible. **Faults**—Spreading toes (splay foot); bent, long toes (rabbit paws); toes turned toward the outside or toward the inside. Furthermore, the fifth toe on the hind legs appearing at a higher position and with wolf's claw or spur; excessively long nails; light-colored nails.

(c) Front End (Shoulders, Legs, Paws)—Shoulders.—The shoulder blades must be strong and sloping and seen from the side, must form as nearly as possible a right angle in its articulation with the humerus (upper arm) to give a long stride. A line from the upper tip of the shoulder to the back of the elbow joint should be as nearly perpendicular as possible. Since all dogs lack a clavicle (collar bone) the ligaments and muscles holding the shoulder blade to the rib cage must be well developed, firm and secure to prevent loose shoulders. **Faults**—Steep shoulders, which occur if the shoulder blade does not slope sufficiently; overangulation; loose shoulders which occur if the Dane is flabby muscled, or if the elbow is turned toward the outside; loaded shoulders.

Forelegs.—The upper arm should be strong and muscular. Seen from the side or front, the strong lower arms run absolutely straight to the pastern joints. Seen from the front, the forelegs and the pastern roots should form perpendicular lines to the ground. Seen from the side, the pastern root should slope only very slightly forward. **Faults**—Elbows turned toward the inside or toward the outside, the former position caused mostly by too narrow or too shallow a chest, bringing the front legs too closely together and at the same time turning the entire lower part of the leg outward; the latter position causes the front legs to spread too far apart, with the pastern roots and paws usually turned inwards. Seen from the side, a considerable bend in the pastern toward the front indicates weakness and is in most cases connected with stretched and spread toes (splay foot); seen from the side, a forward bow in the forearm (chair leg); an excessively knotty bulge in the front of the pastern joint.

Paws.—Round and turned neither toward the inside nor toward the outside. Toes short, highly arched and well closed. Nails short, strong and as dark as possible. **Faults**—Spreading toes (splay foot), bent, long toes (rabbit paws); toes turned toward the outside or toward the inside; lightcolored nails.

3. HEAD

(a) Head Conformation.—Long, narrow, distinguished, expressive, finely chis-

eled, especially the part below the eyes (which means that the skull plane under and to the inner point of the eye must slope without any bony protuberance in a pleasing line to the full square jaw), with strongly pronounced stop. The masculinity of the male is very pronounced in the expression and structure of head (this subtle difference should be evident in the dog's head through massive skull and depth of muzzle); the bitch's head may be more delicately formed. Seen from the side, the forehead must be sharply set off from the bridge of the nose. The forehead and the bridge of the nose must be straight and parallel to one another. Seen from the front, the head should appear narrow, the bridge of the nose should be as broad as possible. The cheek muscles must show slightly, but under no circumstances should they be too pronounced (cheeky). The muzzle part must have full flews and must be as blunt vertically as possible in front; the angles of the lips must be quite pronounced. The front part of the head, from the tip of the nose up to the center of the stop should be as long as the rear part of the head from the center of the stop to the only slightly developed occiput. The head should be angular from all sides and should have definite flat planes and its dimensions should be absolutely in proportion to the general appearance of the Dane. **Faults**—Any deviation from the parallel planes of skull and foreface; too small a stop; a poorly defined stop or none at all; too narrow a nose bridge; the rear of the head spreading laterally in a wedgelike manner (wedge head); an excessively round upper head (apple head); excessively pronounced cheek musculature; pointed muzzle; loose lips hanging over the lower jaw (fluttering lips) which create an illusion of a full deep muzzle. The head should be rather shorter and distinguished than long and expressionless.

(b) Teeth.—Strong, well developed and clean. The incisors of the lower jaw must touch very lightly the bottoms of the inner surface of the upper incisors (scissors bite). If the front teeth of both jaws bite on top of each other, they wear down too rapidly. **Faults**—Even bite; undershot and overshot; incisors out of line; black or brown teeth; missing teeth.

(c) Eyes.—Medium size, as dark as possible, with lively intelligent expression; almond-shaped eyelids,well-developed eyebrows. **Faults**—Light-colored, piercing, amber-colored, light blue to a watery blue, red or bleary eyes; eyes of different colors; eyes too far apart; Mongolian eyes; eyes with pronounced haws; eyes with excessively drooping lower eyelids. In blue and black Danes, lighter eyes are permitted but are not desirable. In harlequins, the eyes should be dark. Light-colored eyes, two eyes of different color and walleyes are permitted but not desirable.

Nose.—The nose must be large and in the case of brindled and "single-colored" Danes, it must always be black. In harlequins, the nose should be black; a black spotted nose is permitted; a pink-colored nose is not desirable.

Ears.—Ears should be high, set not too far apart, medium in size, of moderate thickness, drooping forward close to the cheek. Top line of folded ear should be about level with the skull. **Faults**—Hanging on the side, as on a Foxhound.

Cropped ears: high set, not set too far apart, well pointed but always in proportion to the shape of the head and carried uniformly erect.

4. TORSO

(a) Neck.—The neck should be firm and clean, high-set, well arched, long, muscular and sinewy. From the chest to the head, it should be slightly tapering, beautifully formed, with well-developed nape. **Faults**—Short, heavy neck, pendulous throat folds (dewlaps).

(b) Loin and Back.—The withers forms the highest part of the back which slopes downward slightly toward the loins which are imperceptibly arched and strong. The back should be short and tensely set. The belly should be well shaped and tightly muscled, and, with the rear part of the thorax, should swing in a pleasing curve (tuck-up). **Faults**—Receding back; sway back; camel or roach back; a back line which is too high at the rear; an excessively long back; poor tuck-up.

(c) Chest.—Chest deals with that part of the thorax (rib cage) in front of the shoulders and front legs. The chest should be quite broad, deep and well muscled. **Faults**—A narrow and poorly muscled chest; strong protruding sternum (pigeon breast).

(d) Ribs and Brisket.—Deals with that part of the thorax back of the shoulders and front legs. Should be broad, with the ribs sprung well from the spine and flattened at the side to allow proper movement of the shoulders extending down to the elbow joint. **Faults**—Narrow (slab-sided) rib cage; round (barrel) rib cage; shallow rib cage not reaching the elbow joint.

5. TAIL

Should start high and fairly broad, terminating slender and thin at the hock joint. At rest, the tail should fall straight. When excited or running, slightly curved (saberlike). **Faults**—A too high, or too low set tail (the tail set is governed by the slope of the croup); too long or too short a tail; tail bent too far over the back (ring tail); a tail which is curled; a twisted tail (sideways); a tail carried too high over the back (gay tail); a brush tail (hair too long on lower side). Cropping tails to desired length is forbidden.

DISQUALIFICATIONS

Danes under minimum height.
White Danes without any black marks (albinos).
Merles, a solid mouse-gray color or a mouse-gray base with black or white or both color spots or white base with mouse-gray spots.

Harlequins and solid-colored Danes in which a large spot extends coatlike over the entire body so that only the legs, neck and the point of the tail are white.

Brindle, fawn, blue and black Danes with white forehead line, white collars, high white stockings and white bellies.

Danes with predominantly blue, gray, yellow or also brindled spots.

Any color other than those described under "Color and Markings."

Docked tails.

Split noses.

Approved AUGUST 10, 1976

The German Great Dane Standard

General Appearance and Character.—The Great Dane combines pride, strength and elegance in its noble appearance and big, strong, well-coupled body. It is the Apollo of all the breeds of dogs. The Dane strikes one by its very expressive head; it does not show any nervousness even in the greatest excitement, and has the appearance of a noble statue. In temperament it is friendly, loving and affectionate with its masters, especially with children, but retiring and mistrustful with strangers. In time of danger the dog is courageous and not afraid of attacks, caring only for the defense of its master and the latter's property.

Head.—Elongated, narrow, striking, full of expression, finely chiseled (especially the part under the eyes), with strongly accentuated stop. Seen from the side, the brow should be sharply broken off from the bridge of the nose. The forehead and bridge of the nose must run into each other in a straight and parallel line. Seen from the front, the head must appear narrow, the bridge of the nose must be as broad as possible; the cheek muscles should be only slightly accentuated, but in no case must they be prominent. The muzzle must be full of lip, as much as possible vertically blunted in front, and show well-accentuated lip-angle. The underjaw should be neither protruding nor retrograding. The forehead, from the tip of the nose to the stop, must as far as possible be of the same length as the back of the head, from the stop to the slightly accentuated occiput. Seen from all sides, the head should appear angular and settled in its outer lines, but at the same time it should harmonise entirely with the general appearance of the Great Dane in every way. **Faults:** Falling-off line of brow, an elevated, falling-off or compressed bridge of nose; too little or no stop; too narrow a bridge of nose; the back of the head wedge-shaped; too round a skull (apple head); cheeks too pronounced; snipy muzzle. Also loose lips hanging over the underjaw, which can be deceptive as to a full, deep muzzle. It is preferable for the head to be short and striking, rather than long, shallow and expressionless.

Eyes (in general).—Of medium size, round, as dark as possible, with gay, hearty expression, the eyebrows well developed. **Faults:** Eyes light, cutting, amber-yellow, light blue or water blue, or of two different colors; too low-hanging eyelids with prominent tear glands or very red conjunctiva tunica.

Ears.—Set on high, not too far apart, of good length, cropped to a point. **Faults:** Ears set on too low, laterally; cropped too short or not uniformly; standing too much over or even lying on the head; not carried erect or semi-drooping ears. (Uncropped Danes should not win.) (*Translator's note:* Of course the above refers to cropped ears; with us the ears should be small.)

Nose.—Large, black, running in a straight line with the bridge. **Faults:** Nose light colored, with spots, or cleft.

Teeth.—Large and strong, white, fitting into each other, which is correct when the lower incisors fit tightly into the upper ones just as two scissor blades. **Faults:** The incisors of the lower jaw are protruding (undershot) or those of the upper jaw protrude (overshot). Also, when the incisors of both jaws stand one upon another ('crackers'), for in this case the teeth wear out prematurely. Imperceptible deviations are allowed. Distemper teeth should be objected to as they hide caries; likewise when the teeth look broken or are brown. Tartar is also undesirable.

Neck.—Long, dry, muscular and sinewy, without strongly developed skin or dewlap; it should taper slightly from the chest to the head, be nicely ascending, and set on high with a well-formed nape. **Faults:** Neck short, thick with loose skin or dewlap.

Shoulders.—The shoulder-blade should be long and slanting; it should join the bone of the upper arm in the same position in the shoulder joint, as far as possible forming a right angle, in order to allow roomy movement. The withers should be well accentuated. **Faults:** Straight or loose shoulders; the former occur when the shoulder-blade is not sufficiently slanting, the latter when the elbows turn outwards.

Chest.—As large as possible, the ribs well rounded, deep in front, reaching up to the elbow joints. **Faults:** Chest narrow, shallow with flat ribs; chest bone protruding too much.

Body.—The back straight, short and tight, the body should be as far as possible square in relation to the height; a somewhat longer back is allowed in bitches. The loins should be lightly arched and strong, the croup running fully imperceptibly into the root of the tail. The belly should be well tucked up backwards, and forming a nicely arched line with the inside of the chest. **Faults:** Saddleback, roach-back, or when the height of the hindquarters exceeds that of the forequarters (overbuilt); too long a back, since the gait then suffers (rolling gait); the croup falling off at a slant; belly hanging down and badly showing teats in bitches.

Tail.—Of medium length, only reaching to the hocks, set on high and broad, but tapering to a point; hanging down straight at rest, slightly curved (swordlike) in excitement or in running, not carried over the back. **Faults:** Tail too long, too low set on, carried too high over the back, or curled over the back;

78

turned sideways; broken off or docked (it is forbidden to shorten the tail to obtain the prescribed length); brush tail (when the hair on the inside is too long) is undesirable. It is forbidden to shave the tail.

Front Legs.—The continuation of the elbows of the forearm must not reach the round of the chest, but must be well let down, must not appear either inwards or outwards, but should lie in equal flatness with the shoulder joint. The upper arms should be strong, broad and muscular, the legs strong and—seen from the front or the side—absolutely straight down to the pasterns. **Faults:** Elbows turning in or out; if turning in, their position impedes movement by rubbing against the ribs, and at the same time turns the whole lower part of the legs and causes the feet to turn outwards; if turning out, the reverse happens and the toes are forced inwards. Both these positions are at fault, but the latter does not hinder movement since it does not cause any rubbing of the elbows against the chest wall. If the forelegs stand too wide apart the feet are forced to turn inwards, while in the case of the 'narrow' stand brought about by the narrow chest, the front legs incline towards each other and the toes again turn outwards. The curving of the joint of the root of the front foot is equally faulty; it points to weakness in the pasterns (soft pasterns) or in foot-roots (tarsus), and often causes flat feet and splayed toes. Swelling over the joint of the tarsus points mainly to diseases of the bone (rickets).

Hind Legs.—The buttocks of the hind legs should be broad and muscular, the under-thighs long, strong, and forming a not too obtuse angle with the short tarsus. Seen from behind, the hocks should appear absolutely straight, sloping neither outwards nor inwards. **Faults:** If the knee-joint is turned too far outwards, the under-thigh forces the hock inwards and the dog is then 'cow-hocked,' not a nice position at all. Too broad a stand in the hocks is just as ugly, as it impedes the light movement. In profile, the well-developed hind thigh shows good angulation. A straight hind thigh is faulty, for there the under-thigh is too short and the dog is forced to keep it vertically to the straight tarsus. If the bone of the hind thighs is too long (in relation to the forelimbs), then the hind thighs are diagonally bent together, and this is not at all good.

Feet.—Roundish, turned neither inwards nor outwards. The toes should be short, highly arched and well closed, the nails short, strong and black. **Faults:** Splayed toes, hare-feet, toes turned inwards or outwards; further, the fifth toes on the hind legs placed higher (dew claw); also if the nails are too long, or light in color.

Movement.—Fleeting, stepping out. **Faults:** Short strides which are not free; narrow or rolling gait; ambling gait.

Coat.—Very short and thick, lying close and shiny. **Faults:** Hair too long; lopped hair (due to bad feeding, worms and faulty care).

Color.

(a) Brindle Danes: Ground color from light golden fawn to dark golden fawn, always with well-defined black stripes. The more intense the ground color

and the stronger the stripes, the more striking is the effect. Small white patches on the chest and toes, or light eyes and nails, are not desirable. **Faults:** Silver-blue or biscuit-colored ground color, washed-out stripes, white streak between the eyes up to the nose, white ring on the neck, white 'socks' and white tip of tail. Danes with such white markings should be excluded from winning prizes.

(b) Fawn Danes: Color, fawn-golden and fawn to dark golden fawn; black mask as well as black nails are desired. The golden-fawn color should always be preferred. **Faults:** Silver-grey, blue-grey, biscuit-fawn and dirty-fawn color should be placed lower in the award list. For white markings, see (a) above. (*Translator's note:* It will be seen that whereas a black mask in fawn Great Danes was formerly not desired, as reminding one of Mastiffs, it is now desired.)

(c) Blue Danes: The color should be as far as possible steel blue, without any tinge of fawn or black. Lighter eyes are allowed in blue Danes. **Faults:** Fawn-blue or black-blue color, too light or wall eyes. Regarding white markings, see (a) above.

(d) Black Danes: Should be wallflower black, shiny, with dark eyes and black nails. **Faults:** Yellow-brown or blue-black color; light or amber-colored eyes; lightly colored nails. Danes with too many white markings should be lower in the list of awards. Under white markings it should be noted that a white streak on the throat, spots on the chest, on toes (only up the pasterns) are allowed, but Danes with a white blaze, white ring on the neck, white 'socks' or white belly, should be debarred from winning.

(e) Harlequins: The ground color should always be white, without any spots, with patches running all over the body, well-torn, irregular, wallflower black (a few small grey or brownish patches are admitted but not desired). Nose and nails should be black, but a nose with black spots or a fleshy nose are allowed. Eyes should be dark; light or two-colored eyes are permitted but not desired. **Faults:** White ground color with several large, black patches; bluish-grey ground color; water-light, red or bleary eyes.

The following Danes should be excluded from winning:

1. White Danes without any black markings; albinos, as well as deaf Danes.

2. 'Mantle' harlequins, i.e. Danes having a large patch—like a mantle—running all over the body, and only the legs, neck and tip of the tail are white.

3. So-called 'porcelain' harlequins, i.e. Danes with mostly blue-grey, fawn or even brindle patches.

Size.—The height at the shoulder should not be under 76 cm (1 in. is about 2½ cm), but preferably should measure about 80 cm; in bitches, not under 70 cm but preferably 75 cm and over.

The English Standard

General Appearance.—The Great Dane should be remarkable in size and very muscular, strongly though elegantly built; the head and neck should be carried high, and the tail in line with the back, or slightly upwards but not curled over the hindquarters. Elegance of outline and grace of form are most essential to a Dane; size is absolutely necessary, but there must be that alertness of expression and briskness of movement without which the Dane character is lost. He should have a look of dash and daring, of being ready to go anywhere and do anything. The action should be lithe, springy and free, the hocks move freely and the head be carried high except when galloping.

Head and Skull.—The head, taken altogether, should give the idea of great length and strength of jaw. The muzzle or foreface is broad, and the skull proportionately narrow, so that the whole head, when viewed from above in front, has the appearance of equal breadth throughout. The entire length of head varies with the height of the dog; 13 in. from the tip of the nose to the back of the occiput is a good measurement for a dog of 32 in. at the shoulder. The length from the end of the nose to the point between the eyes should be about equal, or preferably of greater length than from this point to the back of the occiput. The skull should be flat and have a slight indentation running up the centre, the occipital peak not prominent. There should be a decided rise or brow over the eyes but not an abrupt stop between them; the face should be well chiselled, well filled in below the eyes with no appearance of being pinched; the foreface long, of equal depth throughout. The cheeks should show as little lumpiness as possible, compatible with strength. The underline of the head, viewed in profile, should run almost in a straight line from the corner of the lip to the corner of the jawbone, allowing for the fold of the lip, but with no loose skin to hang down. The bridge of the nose should be very wide, with a slight ridge where the cartilage joins the bone. (This is a characteristic of the Breed.) The nostrils should be large, wide and open, giving a blunt look to the nose. A butterfly or flesh-colored nose is not objected to in harlequins. The lips should hang squarely in front, forming a right angle with the upper line of foreface.

Eyes.—Fairly deep set, of medium size and preferably dark. Wall or odd eyes permissible in harlequins.

Ears.—Should be small, set high on the skull and carried slightly erect with the tips falling forward.

Mouth.—The teeth should be level and not project one way or the other.

Neck.—The neck should be long, well arched, and quite clean and free from loose skin, held well up, well set in the shoulders, and the junction of the head and neck well defined.

Forequarters.—The shoulders should be muscular but not loaded, and well sloped back, with the elbows well under the body. The forelegs should be perfectly straight with big bone, which must be flat.

Body.—The body should be very deep, with ribs well sprung and belly well drawn up. The back and loins should be strong, the latter slightly arched.

Hindquarters.—The hindquarters and thighs should be extremely muscular, giving the idea of great strength and galloping power. The second thigh is long and well developed, the stifle and hock well bent, the hocks set low, turning neither in nor out.

Feet.—The feet should be catlike and should not turn in or out. The toes well arched and close, the nails strong and curved. Nails should be black, but light nails are permissible in harlequins.

Tail.—The tail should be thick at the root and taper towards the end, reaching to or just below the hocks. It should be carried in a straight line level with the back, when the dog is in action, slightly curved towards the end, but in no case should it curl or be carried over the back.

Coat.—The hair is short and dense and sleek-looking, and in no case should it be inclined to roughness.

Color.

*(a) **Brindles:*** must be striped, ground color from the lightest yellow to the deepest orange, and the stripes must always be black. Eyes and nails preferably dark.

*(b) **Fawn:*** the color varies from lightest buff to deepest orange, darker shading on the muzzle and ears and around the eyes are by no means objectionable. Eyes and nails preferably dark.

*(c) **Blues:*** the color varies from light grey to deepest slate.

*(d) **Blacks:*** black is black.

(In all the above colors white is only admissible on the chest and feet, but is not desirable even there. The nose is always black (except in blues). Eyes and nails preferably dark.)

*(e) **Harlequins:*** pure white underground, with preferably black patches (blue patches permitted), having the appearance of being torn. In harlequins, wall eyes, pink noses or butterfly noses are permissible but not desirable.

Weight and Size.—The minimum height of an adult dog over eighteen months must be 30 in., that of a bitch 28 in. Weight: the minimum weight of an adult dog over eighteen months should be 120 lb, that of a bitch 100 lb.

Faults.—Cow-hocks. Out at elbows. Straight stifles, Undershot or overshot mouth. Round bone. Snipy muzzle. Straight shoulders. Shell body. Ring tail.

On the following pages the Official Illustrated Standard of The Great Dane Club of America is reproduced by permission of The Great Dane Club of America, and the illustrations are herein printed by special permission of Donald E. Gauthier for the first edition of this book only and are forbidden to be reproduced anywhere else in whole or in part without permission of the copyright holder.

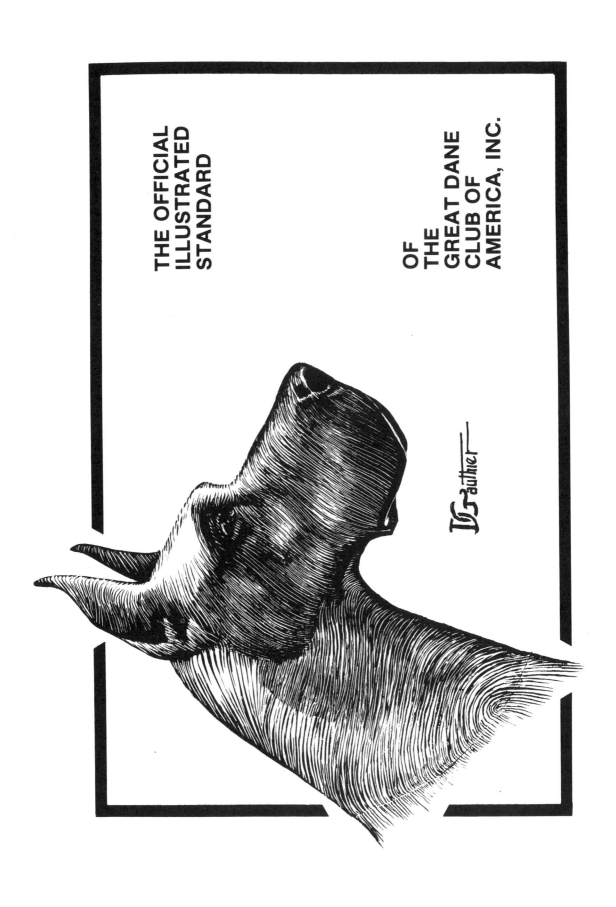

THE OFFICIAL
ILLUSTRATED
STANDARD

OF
THE
GREAT DANE
CLUB OF
AMERICA, INC.

THE OFFICIAL ILLUSTRATED STANDARD
OF THE
GREAT DANE

REVISED AND EDITED BY
THE GREAT DANE CLUB OF AMERICA, INC.

WRITTEN TEXT AKC APPROVED AUGUST 10, 1976

ILLUSTRATED BY

DONALD E. GAUTHIER
GREAT DANE BREEDER AND JUDGE

Copyright, 1972

TABLE OF CONTENTS

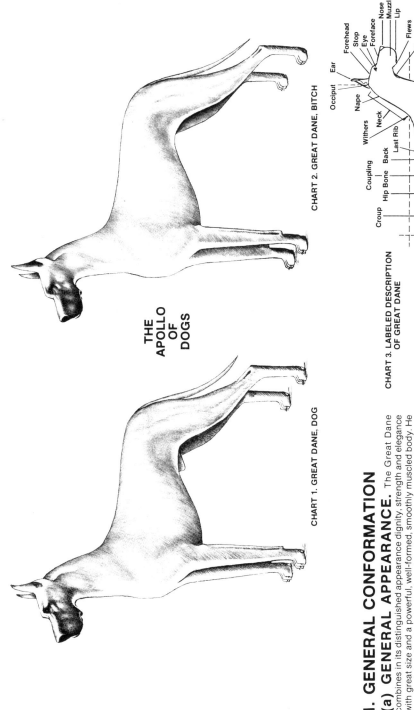

CHART 1. GREAT DANE, DOG

THE
APOLLO
OF
DOGS

CHART 2. GREAT DANE, BITCH

CHART 3. LABELED DESCRIPTION OF GREAT DANE

Labels (Chart 3): Occiput, Ear, Forehead, Stop, Eye, Foreface, Nose, Muzzle, Lip, Flews, Dewlaps, Shoulder, Forechest, Upper Arm, Rib Cage, Forearm, Pastern Joint, Front Pastern, Foot, Nape, Neck, Withers, Last Rib, Back, Coupling, Hip Bone, Croup, Tail Root, Tail, Loin, Tuck Up, Brisket, Elbow, Upper Thigh, Lower Thigh, Hock Joint, Stifle, Rear Pastern, Foot

1. GENERAL CONFORMATION
(a) GENERAL APPEARANCE.
The Great Dane combines in its distinguished appearance dignity, strength and elegance with great size and a powerful, well-formed, smoothly muscled body. He is one of the giant breeds, but is unique in that his general conformation must be so well balanced that he never appears clumsy and is always a unit—the **Apollo of dogs.** He must be spirited and courageous—never timid. He is friendly and dependable. This physical and mental combination is the characteristic which gives the Great Dane the majesty possessed by no other breed. It is particularly true of this breed that there is an impression of great masculinity in dogs as compared to an impression of femininity in bitches. The male should appear more massive throughout than the bitch, with larger frame and heavier bone. In the ratio between length and height, the Great Dane should appear as square as possible. In bitches, a somewhat longer body is permissible.

Faults—Lack of unity; timidity; bitchy dogs; poor musculature; poor bone development; out of condition; rickets; doggy bitches.

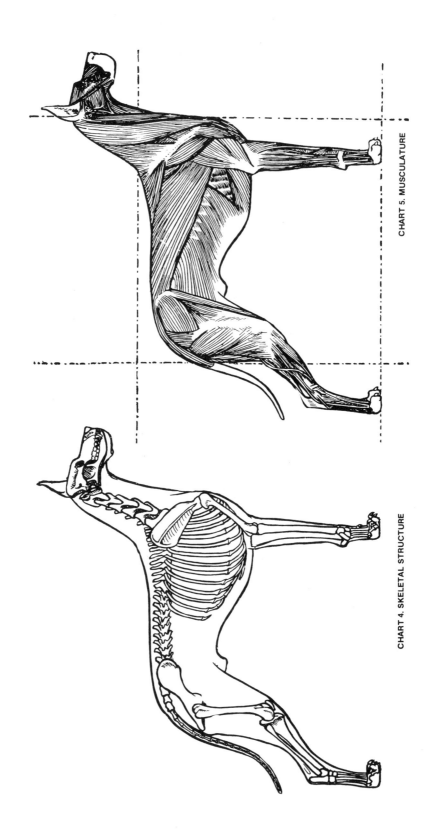

CHART 5. MUSCULATURE

CHART 4. SKELETAL STRUCTURE

(b) COLOR AND MARKINGS

(i) **BRINDLE DANES.** Base color ranging from light golden yellow to deep golden yellow always brindled with strong black cross stripes; deep-black mask preferred. Black may or may not appear on the eyes, ears and tail tip. The more intensive the base color and the more distinct the brindling, the more attractive will be the color. Small white marks at the chest and toes are not desirable. **Faults**—Brindle with too dark a base color, silver-blue and grayish-blue base color; dull (faded) brindlings; white tail tip. Black fronted, dirty colored brindles are not desirable.

(ii) **FAWN DANES.** Light golden yellow to deep golden yellow color with a deep black mask. Black may or may not appear on the eyes, ears, and tail tip. The deep golden yellow color must always be given the preference. Small white spots at the chest and toes are not desirable. **Faults**—Yellowish-gray, bluish-yellow, grayish-blue, dirty yellow color (drab color), lack of black mask. Black fronted, dirty colored fawns are not desirable.

(iii) **BLUE DANES.** The color must be a pure steel blue, as far as possible without any tinge of yellow, black or mouse gray. Small white marks at the chest and toes are not desirable. **Faults**—Any deviation from a pure steel-blue coloration.

(iv) **BLACK DANES.** Glossy Black. **Faults**—Yellow-black, brown-black or blue-black. White markings, such as stripes on the chest, speckled chest and markings on the paws are permitted but not desirable.

(v) **HARLEQUIN DANES.** Base color: pure white with black torn patches irregularly and well distributed over the entire body; pure white neck preferred. The black patches should never be large enough to give the appearance of a blanket nor so small as to give a stippled or dappled effect. (Eligible, but less desirable, are a few small gray spots; also pointings where instead of a pure white base with black spots, there is a white base with single black hairs showing through which tend to give a salt and pepper or dirty effect.) **Faults**—White base color with a few large spots; bluish-gray pointed background.

(c) SIZE.

The male should not be less than 30 inches at the shoulders, but it is preferable that he be 32 inches or more, providing he is well proportioned to his height. The female should not be less than 28 inches at the shoulders, but it is preferable that she be 30 inches or more, providing she is well proportioned to her height.

(d) CONDITION OF COAT.

The coat should be very short and thick, smooth, and glossy. **Faults**—Excessively long hair (stand-off coat); dull hair (indicating malnutrition, worms and negligent care).

(e) SUBSTANCE.

Substance is that sufficiency of bone and muscle which rounds out a balance with the frame. **Faults**—Lightweight whippety Danes; coarse, ungainly proportioned Danes—always there should be balance.

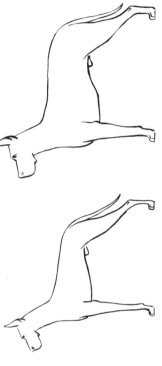

CHART 6. LIGHTWEIGHT WHIPPETY DANE

CHART 7. COARSE DANE

2. MOVEMENT

(a) GAIT.

Long, easy, springy stride with no tossing or rolling of body. The back line should move smoothly, parallel to the ground, with minimum rise and fall. The gait of the Great Dane should denote strength and power showing good driving action in the hindquarters and good reach in front. As speed increases, there is a natural tendency for the legs to converge toward the center line of balance beneath the body and there should be no twisting in or out at the joints.

Faults—Interference or crossing; twisting joints; short steps; stilted steps; the rear quarters should not pitch; the forelegs should not have a hackney gait. When moving rapidly, the Great Dane should not pace for the reason that it causes excessive side-to-side rolling of the body and thus reduces endurance.

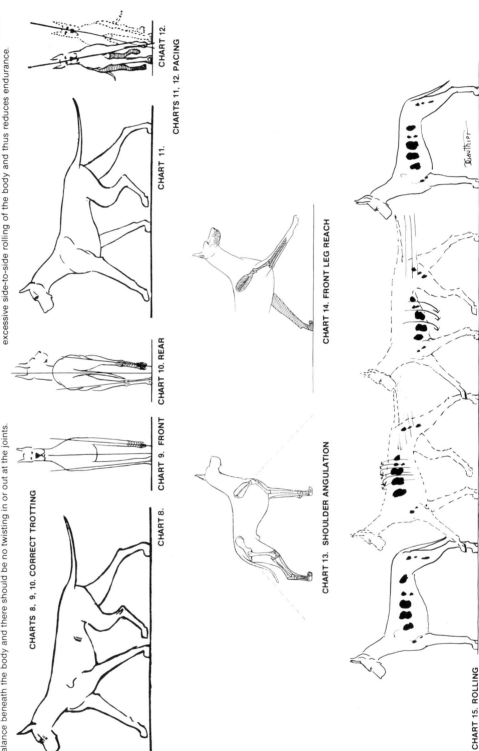

CHART 8.

CHART 9. FRONT

CHART 10. REAR

CHARTS 8, 9, 10. CORRECT TROTTING

CHART 11.

CHART 12.

CHARTS 11, 12. PACING

CHART 13. SHOULDER ANGULATION

CHART 14. FRONT LEG REACH

CHART 15. ROLLING

(b) REAR END
CROUP, LEGS, PAWS

The croup must be full, slightly drooping and must continue imperceptibly to the tail root.

Faults—A croup which is too straight; a croup which slopes downward too steeply; and too narrow a croup.

Hind legs, the first thighs (from hip joint to knee) are broad and muscular. The second thighs (from knee to hock joint) are strong and long. Seen from the side, the angulation of the first thigh with the body, of the second thigh with the first thigh, and the pastern root with the second thigh should be very moderate, neither too straight nor too exaggerated. Seen from the rear, the hock joints appear to be perfectly straight, turned neither towards the inside nor towards the outside.

Faults—Hind legs: Soft flabby, poorly muscled thighs; cowhocks which are the result of the hock joint turning inward and the hock and rear paws turning outward; barrel legs, the result of the hock joints being too far apart; steep rear. As seen from the side, a steep rear is the result of the angles of the rear legs forming almost a straight line; overangulation is the result of exaggerated angles between the first and second thighs and the hocks and is very conducive to weakness. The rear legs should never be too long in proportion to the front legs.

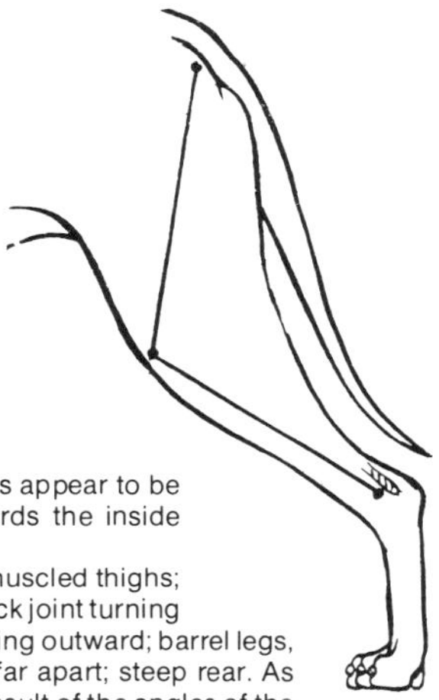

CHART 16. CORRECT ANGULATION

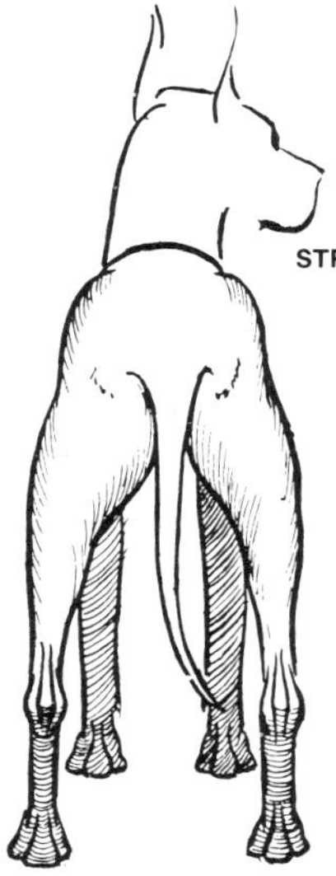

CHART 17. CORRECT REAR

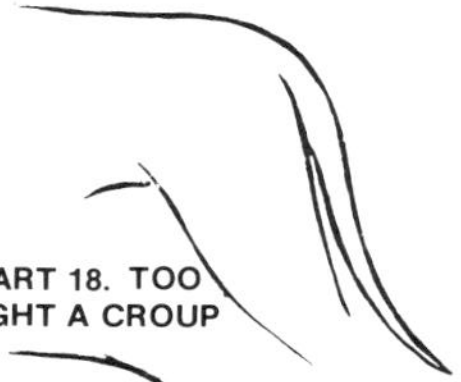

CHART 18. TOO STRAIGHT A CROUP

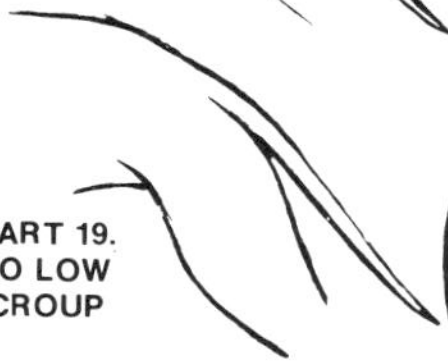

CHART 19. TOO LOW A CROUP

CHART 20. NARROW CROUP

CHART 21. COW HOCKS

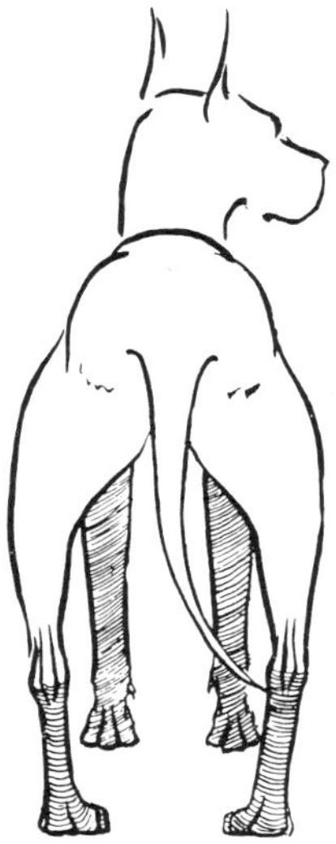

CHART 22. BARREL-LEG REAR

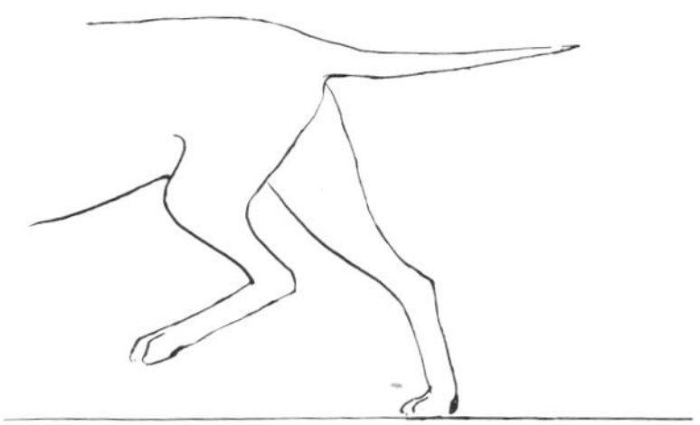

CHART 23. CORRECT FLEXING

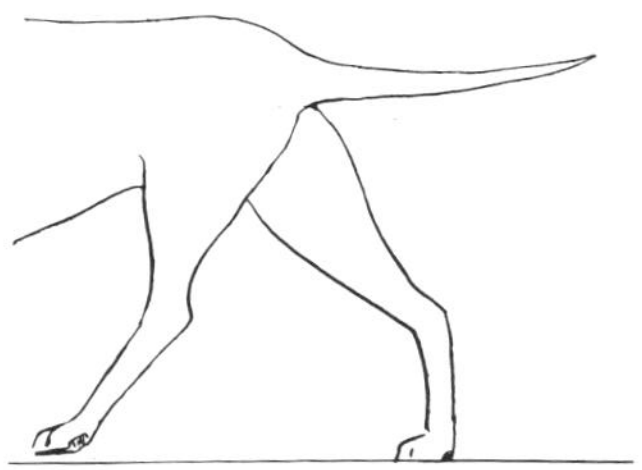

CHART 24. INCORRECT, LACK OF FLEXING

CHART 25. STRAIGHT STEEP REAR, LACKING ANGULATION

CHART 26. EXAGGERATED ANGULATION

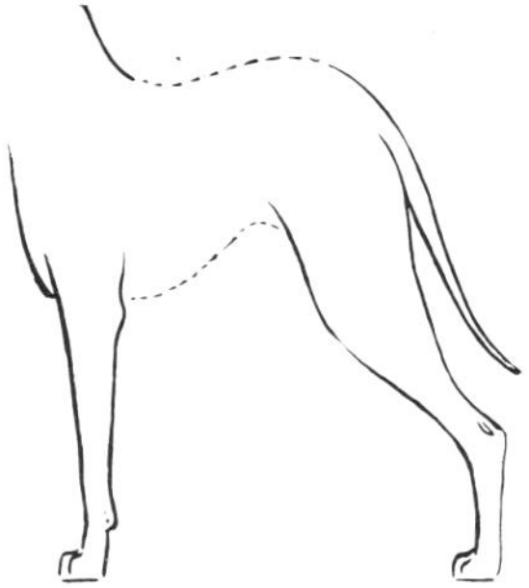

CHART 27. REAR LEGS TOO HIGH

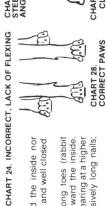

CHART 28. CORRECT PAWS

CHART 29. WELL CLOSED PAW

CHART 30. WELL ARCHED PAW

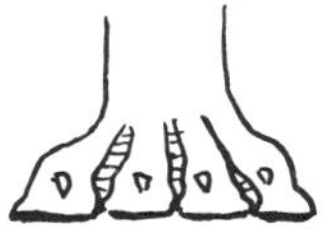

CHART 31. SPLAY FOOT

CHART 32. RABBIT FOOT

PAWS. Round and turned neither toward the inside nor toward the outside. Toes short, highly arched and well closed. Nails short, strong and as dark as possible.

Faults—Spreading toes (splay foot); bent, long toes (rabbit paws); toes turned toward the outside or toward the inside. Furthermore, the fifth toe on the hind legs appearing at a higher position and with wolf's claw or spur; excessively long nails; light-colored nails.

(c) FRONT END SHOULDERS, LEGS, PAWS

SHOULDERS. The shoulder blades must be strong and sloping and seen from the side, must form as nearly as possible a right angle in its articulation with the humerus (upper arm) to give a long stride. A line from the upper tip of the shoulder to the back of the elbow joint should be as nearly perpendicular as possible. Since all dogs lack clavicle (collar bone) the ligaments and muscles holding the shoulder blade to the rib cage must be well developed, firm and secure to prevent loose shoulders.

Faults—Steep shoulders, which occur if the shoulder blade does not slope sufficiently; overangulation; loose shoulders which occur if the Dane is flabby muscled, or if the elbow is turned toward the outside; loaded shoulders.

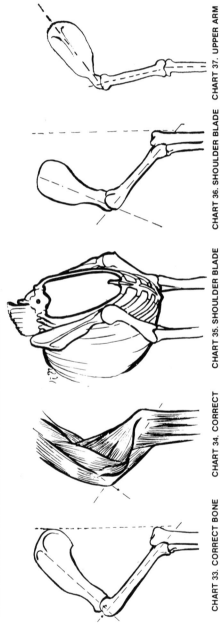

CHART 33. CORRECT BONE STRUCTURE AND ANGULATION

CHART 34. CORRECT MUSCLE STRUCTURE

CHART 35. SHOULDER BLADE STRUCTURE

CHART 36. SHOULDER BLADE TOO STEEP

CHART 37. UPPER ARM TOO SHORT, SHOULDER TOO STRAIGHT

CHART 38. OVERANGULATION

PAWS. Round and turned neither toward the inside nor toward the outside. Toes short, highly arched and well closed. Nails short, strong and as dark as possible.

Faults—Spreading toes (splay foot), bent, long toes (rabbit paws); toes turned toward the outside or toward the inside; light-colored nails.

CHART 39. PAWS TURNED OUT

CHART 40. PAWS TURNED IN

CHART 41. WOLF'S CLAW

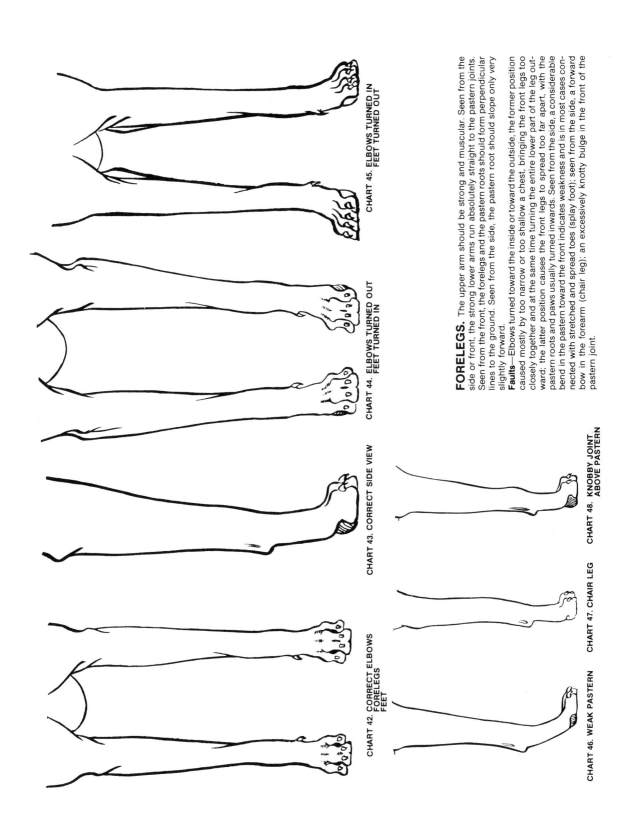

CHART 45. ELBOWS TURNED IN
FEET TURNED OUT

CHART 44. ELBOWS TURNED OUT
FEET TURNED IN

CHART 43. CORRECT SIDE VIEW

CHART 42. CORRECT ELBOWS
FORELEGS
FEET

CHART 48. KNOBBY JOINT
ABOVE PASTERN

CHART 47. CHAIR LEG

CHART 46. WEAK PASTERN

FORELEGS. The upper arm should be strong and muscular. Seen from the side or front, the strong lower arms run absolutely straight to the pastern joints. Seen from the front, the forelegs and the pastern roots should form perpendicular lines to the ground. Seen from the side, the pastern root should slope only very slightly forward.

Faults—Elbows turned toward the inside or toward the outside, the former position caused mostly by too narrow or too shallow a chest, bringing the front legs too closely together and at the same time turning the entire lower part of the leg outward; the latter position causes the front legs to spread too far apart, with the pastern roots and paws usually turned inwards. Seen from the side, a considerable bend in the pastern toward the front indicates weakness and is in most cases connected with stretched and spread toes (splay foot); seen from the side, a forward bow in the forearm (chair leg); an excessively knotty bulge in the front of the pastern joint.

3. HEAD

(a) HEAD CONFORMATION.

Long, narrow, distinguished, expressive, finely chiseled, especially the part below the eyes (which means that the skull plane under and to the inner point of the eye must slope without any bony protuberance in a pleasing line to the full square jaw), with strongly pronounced stop. The masculinity of the male is very pronounced in the expression and structure of head (this subtle difference should be evident in the dog's head through massive skull and depth of muzzle); the bitch's head may be more delicately formed. Seen from the side, the forehead must be sharply set off from the bridge of the nose. The forehead and the bridge of the nose must be straight and parallel to one another. Seen from the front, the head should appear narrow, the bridge of the nose should be as broad as possible. The cheek muscles must show slightly, but under no circumstances should they be too pronounced (cheeky). The muzzle part must have full flews and must be as blunt vertically as possible in front; the angles of the lips must be quite pronounced. The front part of the head, from the tip of the nose up to the center of the stop should be as long as the rear part of the head from the center of the stop to the only slightly developed occiput. The head should be angular from all sides and should have definite flat planes and its dimensions should be absolutely in proportion to the general appearance of the Dane.

Faults—Any deviation from the parallel planes of skull and foreface; too small a stop; a poorly defined stop or none at all; too narrow a nose bridge; the rear of the head spreading laterally in a wedgelike manner (wedge head); an excessively round upper head (apple head); excessively pronounced cheek musculature; pointed muzzle; loose lips hanging over the lower jaw (fluttering lips) which create an illusion of a full deep muzzle. The head should be rather shorter and distinguished than long and expressionless.

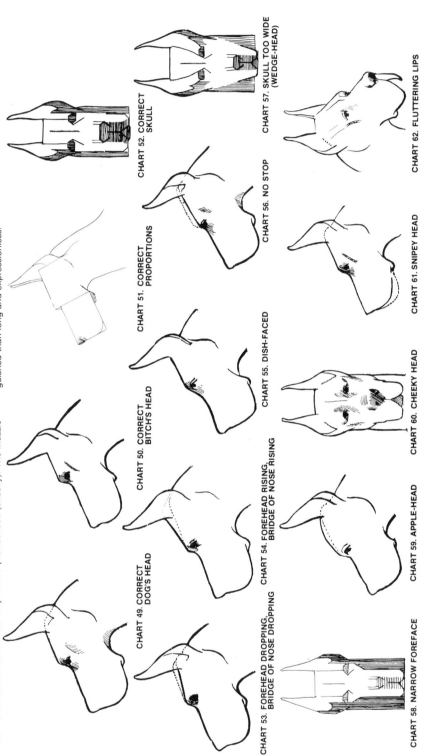

CHART 49. CORRECT DOG'S HEAD

CHART 50. CORRECT BITCH'S HEAD

CHART 51. CORRECT PROPORTIONS

CHART 52. CORRECT SKULL

CHART 53. FOREHEAD DROPPING, BRIDGE OF NOSE DROPPING

CHART 54. FOREHEAD RISING, BRIDGE OF NOSE RISING

CHART 55. DISH-FACED

CHART 56. NO STOP

CHART 57. SKULL TOO WIDE (WEDGE-HEAD)

CHART 58. NARROW FOREFACE

CHART 59. APPLE-HEAD

CHART 60. CHEEKY HEAD

CHART 61. SNIPEY HEAD

CHART 62. FLUTTERING LIPS

(b) TEETH.
Strong, well developed and clean. The incisors of the lower jaw must touch very lightly the bottoms of the inner surface of the upper incisors (scissors bite). If the front teeth of both jaws bite on the top of each other, they wear down too rapidly.

Faults—Even bite; undershot and overshot; incisors out of line; black or brown teeth; missing teeth.

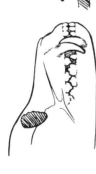

CHART 63. CORRECT SCISSOR BITE

CHART 64. EVEN BITE

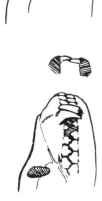

CHART 65. UNDERSHOT

CHART 66. OVERSHOT

(c) EYES.
Medium size, as dark as possible, with lively intelligent expression; almond-shaped eyelids, well-developed eyebrows.

Faults—Light-colored, piercing, amber-colored, light blue to a watery blue, red or bleary eyes; eyes of different colors; eyes too far apart; Mongolian eyes; eyes with pronounced haws; eyes with excessively drooping lower eyelids. In blue and black Danes, lighter eyes are permitted but are not desirable. In harlequins, the eyes should be dark. Light-colored eyes, two eyes of different color and walleyes are permitted but not desirable.

CHART 67. CORRECT EYES

CHART 68. WIDE-SPREAD EYES

CHART 69. MONGOLIAN EYE

CHART 70. CORRECT EYE

CHART 71. HAW

CHART 72. DROOPING LOWER EYELIDS

NOSE.
The nose must be large and in the case of brindled and "single-colored" Danes, it must always be black. In harlequins, the nose should be black; a black spotted nose is permitted; a pink-colored nose is not desirable.

CHART 73. CORRECT NOSE

CHART 74. SPLIT NOSE

EAR MUSCULATURE

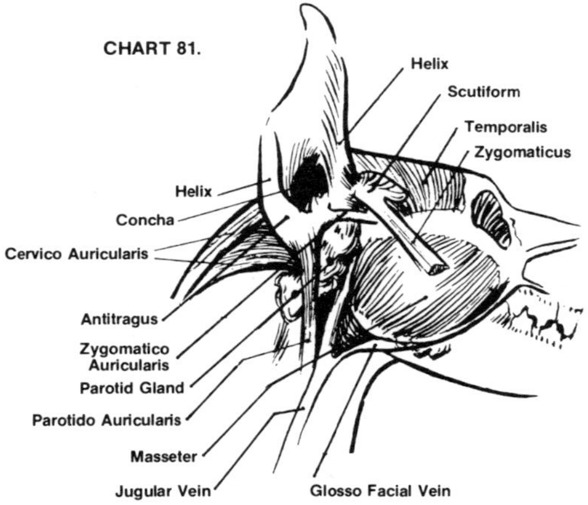

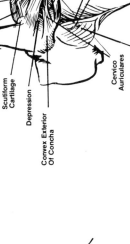

Helix
Scutiform
Temporalis
Zygomaticus

Helix

Concha

Cervico Auricularis

Antitragus

Zygomatico Auricularis

Parotid Gland

Parotido Auricularis

Masseter

Jugular Vein

Glosso Facial Vein

CHART 81.

Temporo Auricularis

Scutiform Cartilage

Depression

Convex Exterior Of Concha

Cervico Auricularis

Mastoid Protruberance

Jugular Vein

Parotid Gland

Cervico Auriculares

Masseter Muscle

CHART 82.

EARS. Ears should be high, set not too far apart, medium in size, of moderate thickness, drooping forward close to the cheek. Top line of folded ear should be about level with the skull.
Faults—Hanging on the side, as on a Foxhound.

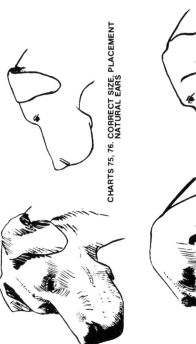

CHARTS 75, 76. CORRECT SIZE, PLACEMENT NATURAL EARS

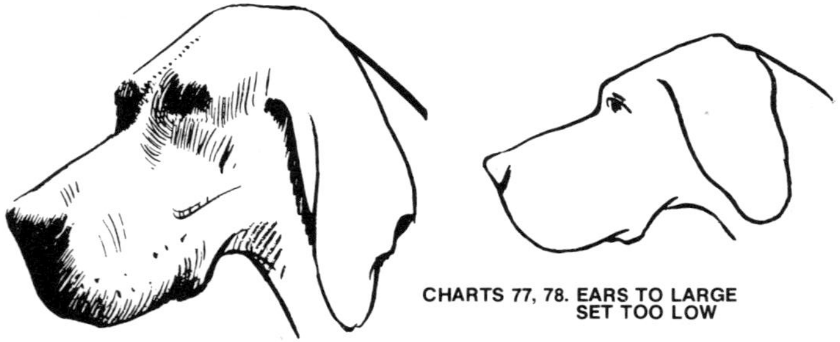

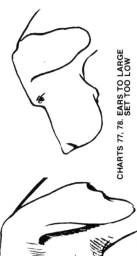

CHARTS 77, 78. EARS TO LARGE SET TOO LOW

CROPPED EARS. High set, not set too far apart, well pointed but always in proportion to the shape of the head and carried uniformly erect.

CHART 79. CROPPED EARS, CORRECT SET　　**CHART 80. CROPPED EARS, SET TOO LOW**

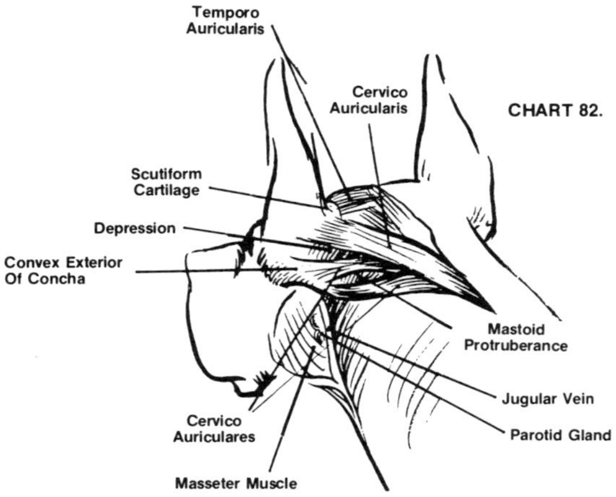

NECK MUSCULATURE

TORSO

(a) NECK.

The neck should be firm and clean, high-set, well arched, long, muscular and sinewy. From the chest to the head, it should be slightly tapering, beautifully formed, with well-developed nape.

Faults—Short, heavy neck, pendulous throat folds (dewlaps).

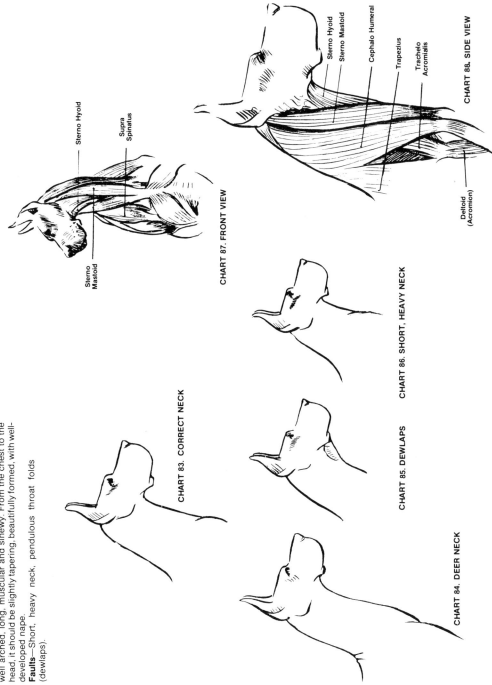

Sterno Hyoid

Supra Spinatus

Sterno Mastoid

CHART 87. FRONT VIEW

Sterno Hyoid

Sterno Mastoid

Cephalo Humeral

Trapezius

Trachelo Acromialis

Deltoid (Acromion)

CHART 88. SIDE VIEW

CHART 83. CORRECT NECK

CHART 84. DEER NECK

CHART 85. DEWLAPS

CHART 86. SHORT, HEAVY NECK

(b) LOIN AND BACK. The withers forms the highest part of the back which slopes downward slightly toward the loins which are imperceptibly arched and strong. The back should be short and tensely set. The belly should be well shaped and tightly muscled, and, with the rear part of the thorax, should swing in a pleasing curve (tuck-up).

Faults—Receding back; sway back; camel or roach back; a back line which is too high at the rear, an excessively long back; poor tuck-up.

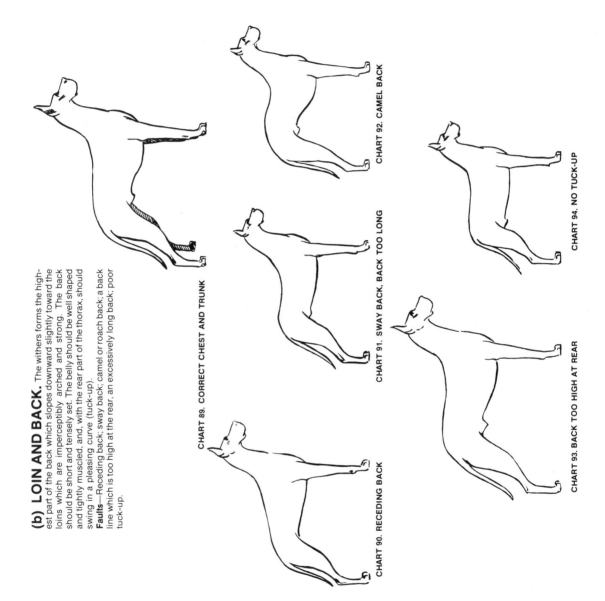

CHART 89. CORRECT CHEST AND TRUNK

CHART 90. RECEDING BACK

CHART 91. SWAY BACK, BACK TOO LONG

CHART 92. CAMEL BACK

CHART 93. BACK TOO HIGH AT REAR

CHART 94. NO TUCK-UP

(c) CHEST. Chest deals with that part of the thorax (rib cage) in front of the shoulders and front legs. The chest should be quite broad, deep and well muscled.

Faults—A narrow and poorly muscled chest; strong protruding sternum (pigeon breast).

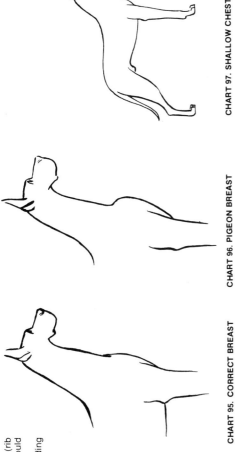

CHART 95. CORRECT BREAST

CHART 96. PIGEON BREAST

CHART 97. SHALLOW CHEST

(d) RIBS AND BRISKET. Deals with that part of the thorax back of the shoulders and front legs. Should be broad, with the ribs sprung well out from the spine and flattened at the side to allow proper movement of the shoulders extending down to the elbow joint.

Faults—Narrow (slab-sided) rib cage; round (barrel) rib cage; shallow rib cage not reaching the elbow joint.

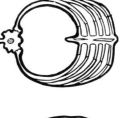

CHART 101. BARREL RIB CAGE

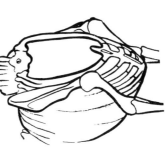

CHART 100. NARROW RIB CAGE

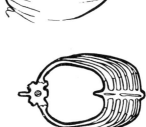

CHART 99. RIB CAGE AND SHOULDER BLADE STRUCTURE

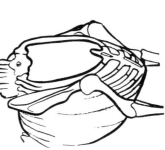

CHART 98. CORRECT RIB CAGE

5. TAIL

Should start high and fairly broad, terminating slender and thin at the hock joint. At rest, the tail should fall straight. When excited or running, slightly curved (saberlike).

Faults—A too high, or too low set tail (the tail set is governed by the slope of the croup); too long or too short a tail; tail bent too far over the back (ring tail); a tail which is curled; a twisted tail (sideways); tail carried too high over the back (gay tail); a brush tail (hair too long on lower side). Cropping tails to desired length is forbidden.

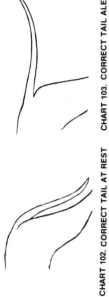

CHART 102. CORRECT TAIL AT REST

CHART 103. CORRECT TAIL ALERT

CHART 104. TOO HIGH SET TAIL

CHART 105. TOO LOW SET TAIL

CHART 106. TOO LONG A TAIL

CHART 107. TOO SHORT A TAIL

CHART 108. RING TAIL

CHART 109. CURLY TAIL

CHART 110. TWISTED TAIL

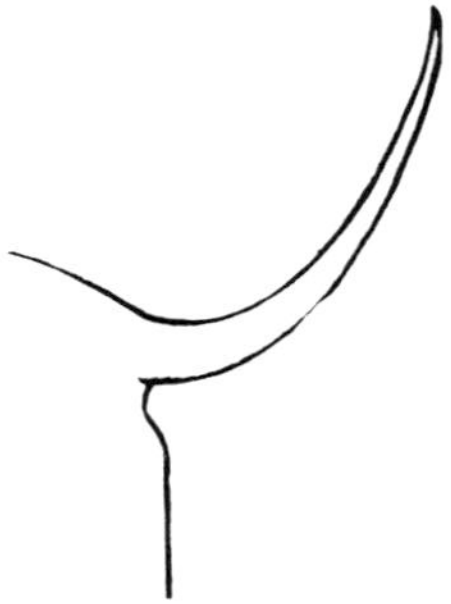

CHART 111. GAY TAIL

9

Color Code of Ethics for the Great Dane Breeder

T HE "CODE" on the next page is meant to be a guideline for breeders.

The Color Research Committee of The Great Dane Club of America reported in 1970 that breeding practices had shown a marked regression due to a laxity in following the then existing code. We had a situation developing that had not existed since the early 1900's or in Germany since before the end of the 1800's when the Germans developed a strict code.

In *Die Deutsche Dogge* published in 1887 there are two paragraphs entitled Color and Markings:

BREEDERS CODE OF ETHICS

as endorsed by
THE GREAT DANE CLUB OF AMERICA

There are only five recognized colors; all these basically fall into four color strains: 1. FAWN and BRINDLE, 2. HARLEQUIN and HARLEQUIN BRED BLACK, 3. BLUE and BLUE BRED BLACK, 4. BLACK. Color classifications being well founded, the Great Dane Club of America, Inc. considers it an inadvisable practice to mix color strains and it is the club's policy to adhere only to the following matings:

Color of Dane	Pedigree of Sire and Dam	Approved Breedings
1. FAWN	Four (4) generation Pedigrees of FAWN or BRINDLE Danes *should not* carry BLACK, HARLEQUIN or BLUE upon them.	1. FAWN bred to FAWN or BRINDLE only.
1. BRINDLE		1. BRINDLE bred to BRINDLE or FAWN only.
2. HARLEQUIN	Four (4) Generation Pedigrees of HARLEQUIN or HARLEQUIN BRED BLACK Danes *should not* carry FAWN, BRINDLE or BLUE upon them.	2. HARLEQUIN bred to HARLEQUIN, BLACK from HARLEQUIN BREEDING or BLACK from BLACK BREEDING only.
2. BLACK (HARLEQUIN BRED)		2. BLACK from HARLEQUIN BREEDING bred to HARLEQUIN, BLACK from HARLEQUIN BREEDING or BLACK from BLACK BREEDING only.
3. BLUE	Four (4) Generation Pedigrees of BLUE or BLUE BRED BLACK Danes *should not* carry FAWN, BRINDLE or HARLEQUIN upon them.	3. BLUE bred to BLUE, BLACK from BLUE BREEDING or BLACK from BLACK BREEDING only.
3. BLACK (BLUE BRED)		3. BLACK from BLUE BREEDING bred to BLUE, BLACK from BLUE BREEDING or BLACK from BLACK BREEDING only.
4. BLACK (BLACK BRED)	Four (4) Generation Pedigrees of BLACK BRED Danes *should not* carry FAWN, BRINDLE, HARLEQUIN or BLUE upon them.	4. BLACK from BLACK BREEDING bred to BLACK, BLUE or HARLEQUIN only. *(See note below.)*

Note: Black Bred Great Danes may be bred to Blacks, Blues or Harlequins only; Puppies resulting from these breedings will become Blacks or Harlequins from Harlequin breeding (category 2 above), Blacks or Blues from Blue breeding (category 3 above) or Blacks from Black Breeding (category 4 above).

It is our belief that color mixing other than that set forth above is injurious to our breed.

ALL COLORS SHALL BE PURE COLOR BRED FOR FOUR (4) GENERATIONS

"The recognized colors are, the various shades of grey (commonly termed 'blue'), red, black, or pure white, or white with patches of the before-mentioned colors. These colors are sometimes accompanied with markings of a darker tint about the eyes and muzzle, and with a line of the same tint (called a 'trace') along the course of the spine. The above ground colors also appear in the brindles, and are also the ground colors of the mottled specimens. In the whole-colored specimens, the china or wall eye but rarely appears and the nose more or less approaches black, according to the prevailing tint of the dog, and the eyes vary in color also.

"The mottled specimens have irregular patches or 'clouds' upon the above-named ground colors; in some instances the clouds or markings being of two or more tints. With the mottled specimens the wall or china eye is not uncommon, and the nose is often parti-colored or wholly flesh-colored."

As breeders we do not need to have these colors reappear across the country. Therefore, in its wisdom the Parent Club set down the revised Code. As a result, there are today many blue, black and harlequin lines that have been cleared sufficiently so that an updating to five generations pure color bred could probably take place, and most fawn and brindle lines are once again five, six or more generations pure color bred.

A sincere breeder interested in establishing and maintaining a pure color line will benefit by strictly adhering to the Code of Ethics.

10

The Genetics of Coat Color in the Great Dane

by Kenneth A. Doeg, Ph.D.

As with other complex features of the anatomy of the dog, color and coat pattern are controlled not by one but by a series of genes, each of which exerts its own action and interacts with the others to alter and modify the coat color and pattern. Most of the information in this chapter comes from the work of Dr. Clarence Little, former Director of the Jackson Memorial Laboratories, Bar Harbor, Maine, where most of this work was done. This is not to deny the considerable contributions of other geneticists over the years but it was the work of Little which brought our knowledge of coat color in dogs to the stage at which it now rests. Very few people are working in this field today. Most of the modern coat color work is being done with mice, rats, guinea pigs and rabbits, animals that are much easier than dogs to feed, care for and breed in large numbers. We can surmise a good deal of information about the dog from this work since the coat color genes have been shown to be substantially the same in all mammals. However, it is the framework provided by the work of Little that permits us to make these jumps between other mammals and the dog. A reference to the book summarizing his work is found at the end of this chapter.

Five basic color-pattern combinations are accepted in the show ring according to the American Great Dane Standard. The accepted colors are fawn, brindle, black, blue and harlequin. Leather, mask and nails in the fawn and leather, mask, nails and stripes in the brindle must be black. The black and blue Dane must not carry excessive amounts of white and, when present, must be largely restricted to the chest and toes. The white restriction also applies to the fawn and brindle. The harlequin is basically a white dog with well-distributed black patches. An occasional merle (blue-grey) spot on the harlequin is acceptable. For a more complete description of the accepted colors, see the Standard in chapter 8 of this book.

Other colors and patterns have been recorded for the Great Dane, none of which can be shown in the conformation ring. Therefore, if a person is seriously interested in showing and producing top quality Great Danes, it is necessary to know enough about coat color genetics to permit the purchase of proper breeding stock and the choice of the best dams and studs to breed from. This insures that the progeny produced will have the best chance of being show quality animals. Remember, no matter how excellent in conformation a Great Dane is, it will be disqualified by any knowledgeable judge if it does not meet the color criteria in the standard.

The known genes that control coat color in the dog comprise nine series. They are *A, B, C, D, E, G, M, S* and *T* gene series. Variations in all but the *G* and *T* series determine coat color patterns in the Dane. It must be pointed out at this stage that all of these genes are present in all dogs although different ones vary in different breeds. Undoubtedly a number more that we either don't know anything about or enough about to include here exist. From the variability in harlequin pattern and the variety in intensity we see in fawn base color, brindling and depth of mask, this is a safe prediction. This chapter will present the role of the various genes listed and, if the reader can keep them all together, most of the coat colors we see in the Great Dane today can be easily explained. There are some really tough ones that the Color Research Committee of the Great Dane Club of America has been grappling with but these need not concern us in the chapter. Each gene will be discussed in turn. As each is introduced, when one gene interacts with another to alter coat color, that fact will be noted and the consequences to coat color will be pointed out. The situation in fawns, brindles, blacks and blues will be dealt with first since these are the easiest to understand. After these genes are well in hand, we will add those genes that go into making the harlequin, merle and Boston coat color patterns. To begin with, it is well to remember that two kinds of gene action are dealt with here, those which produce the pigment and those which tell the body mechanisms where to put the color made. Try to keep these categories in mind as you read further.

The *B* gene series

We are starting with the *B* series since this is probably the easiest gene series to understand. The gene in dominant form (*B*) signals the body to make black pigment. Where the black pigment will be is determined by other genes so this gene says black in the fawn mask, leather and nails, in the brindle stripes, mask, nails and leather, in the overall black in the black and blue (dilute black, see the *D* gene) and in the black spots of the harlequin. Its partner (*b*) causes the production of chocolate or liver color but only in double dose (*bb*) and is a perfectly respectable gene in many breeds of dog. Because the animals with the color produced by this gene (*bb*) are not of show quality in Danes, it is well we know about it. Since the *B* is dominant and the *b* is recessive, a Dane with black can be either *BB* or *Bb*. A chocolate must be *bb*.

The *A* gene series

This is one of the location or pattern genes referred to earlier. It instructs the body where to place the pigment, made under the control of other genes like the *B* series. There are four genes in this series, only two of which are found—except perhaps very rarely—in Danes. Those found are the A^s and the a^y. The A^s instructs that the color produced is to be spread all over the animal (the small white spots seen on the chest and toes are produced by another gene). The "*s*" in the A^s refers to self-color, a term meaning an animal with all-over pigment like the Irish Setter, the Labrador Retriever and the black Dane. A^s is dominant over a^y, so a self-colored Dane can be either A^sA^s or A^sa^y. The gene a^y restricts the black or chocolate color produced by the *B* gene series to small areas and leaves behind a yellow (the *y* in a^y) that we call fawn. Brindles are also a^ya^y which accounts for their fawn ground color. Their stripes and masking as well as the masking of the fawn is determined by yet another

The color BLACK is well represented by Can. Ch. Willowrun's Tomterific V RVRWD.

The color BLUE is well represented by Azurs Elbina, owned by Mrs. Pat Haltmeier.

The color HARLEQUIN is well represented by Ch. Riverwood's Marko Polo.

The color BRINDLE is well represented by Ch.
Regency's Rebecca.

The color FAWN is well represented by Sir
Brian Boru of Magnus.

gene series, the E series, which will come later. The two genes in this series that are rarely found in the Dane are the a^t and the a^w. In double dose, $a^t a^t$ produces the tan point pattern we see in Doberman Pinschers and in Basenjis among others. The a^w is very rare and produces the wild (grey) color in wolves. It is occasionally seen in the German Shepherd Dog. At a recent show in the northeast, a tan-point Dane (a blue with tan-point pattern much like a blue Doberman Pinscher) was seen at ringside. The owner claimed the dog came from blue to blue breeding with a clear pedigree for many generations.

Let's try a few questions on coat color now so you can test yourself on your comprehension up to this point. If you have difficulty with two genes, you will be completely lost as more and more are piled on, so if you can't answer or don't understand the answers to the questions posed, do go back and reread the sections on the A and B gene series.

1. Write the genetic formula using the A and B gene series for a fawn with black where black is supposed to be.
   Ans.: $a^y a^y B*$ * either B or b here, you can't tell unless you breed.

2. Write the genetic formula using the A and B series for a black dog. To make it easier, let's say there is no fawn in the background.
   Ans.: $A^s A^s B*$ * same as above

3. Write the genetic formula for a black stud and a black bitch which, when bred, produced a litter of black and fawn puppies.
   Ans.: $A^s a^y B?$ $\times$ $A^s a^y B?$ If fawns ($a^y a^y$) are to be produced, both the stud and the bitch must have one a^y. They each must also have A^s to make them black.

The E gene series

There are four genes in this series: E^m-mask, E-solid light coat color, no mask, e^{br}-brindling and e-coat restricted to yellow-red. E is short for extension (of color), and is another one of these pattern genes. There is a question as to whether the e gene is ever found in the Dane so to make things easier, this gene will be disregarded. Some breeds of dogs are fawn or red because they are ee; the Dane is fawn because he is $a^y a^y$. This will take care of 99.999% of all fawns in Danes.

The genes in this series are a good example of co-dominance; i.e., the genes of a pair have equal activities and one does not cover up the effects of the other as in the B,b example. One dose of the E^m gene confers a mask on a fawn or a brindle. One dose of e^{br} changes what would be a fawn into a brindle. A brindle with a mask would then be $E^m e^{br}$. Both genes are acting at the same time and the action of both can be seen. EE will produce a fawn without a mask, a fault in the United States but actually preferred at least by some in England where they are called golden fawns. More than one fawn without mask has been finished in the United State since it is a fault but not a disqualification and, in an otherwise excellent animal, need not be penalized too heavily. A fawn with a mask, then, could be $E^m E^m$ or $E^m E$.

Let's see now whether the three genes and their actions are firmly fixed in your memory registers with some more problems.

   5. Write the genetic formula for a brindle with a black mask using the genes of the A, B, and E series.
      Ans.: $a^y a^y B\underline{?}\ E^m e^{br}$

   6. Write the genetic formula for a chocolate brindle with a mask.
      Ans.: $a^y a^y bb E^m e^{br}$

   7. Write the genetic formula for a brindle stud or dam that can only throw brindle puppies. What can you tell about the color of his or her parents?
      Ans.: $a^y a^y e^{br} e^{br} B\underline{?}\ $ Both parents must have been brindles since one of each of the pair of e^{br} must have come from each parent.

   8. Write the genetic formula for a *brindle* dam and a *fawn* sire both with mask and normal color but that have produced a litter containing chocolate fawns and chocolate brindle puppies.
      Ans.: $a^y a^y Bb E^m e^{br}$ × $a^y a^y Bb E^m \underline{?}\ $ Each parent must have one b
            (dam)   (sire)   gene for chocolate puppies to result.

It should be noted before we leave the E gene series that the effects of the E genes can only be seen in the presence of $a^y a^y$. This combination gives the fawn background upon which the E genes can act. However, don't think for a moment that these E genes can't exist in a black or blue dog. They are there: you just can't see their action. To illustrate what can happen when many colors are represented in a pedigree, let's take the case of a black dog with two brindle grandparents bred to a normal fawn and then an inbreeding with the progeny from that cross. For simplicity, let's assume that both have a double dose of the B gene so we can assume that any progeny will be BB. The black dog is $A^s A^s e^{br} e^{br}$ and the fawn dam is a $a^y a^y E^m E^m$. The black sire is really a black brindle but the stripes can't be seen behind that solid black color. Figure 1 shows the genetic content of the sex cells and the various ways in which they can recombine. Note that, although there are 12:16 chances of producing

110

black dogs from this cross, in the F_2 generation, the black dogs are very different genetically and can throw very different things genetically to their next generation.

Parental generation: $A^sA^se^{br}e^{br} \times a^ya^yE^mE^m$

(sire)   (dam)

Parental sex cells: $A^se^{br} \times a^yE^m$ (only one type for each)

First filial generation: $A^sa^yE^me^{br}$ black but carries mask and brindling genes

F_1 inbred cross: $A^sa^yE^me^{br} \times A^sa^yE^me^{br}$

F_1 sex cells: A^sE^m, A^se^{br}, a^yE^m, a^ye^{br} for both (4 possible combinations for each)

F_2 generation:

	A^sE^m	A^se^{br}	a^yE^m	a^ye^{br}
	1	2	3	4
A^sE^m	$A^sA^sE^mE^m$	$A^sA^se^{br}E^m$	$a^yA^sE^mE^m$	$a^yA^se^{br}E^m$
	5	6	7	8
A^se^{br}	$A^sA^sE^me^{br}$	$A^sA^se^{br}e^{br}$	$a^yA^sE^me^{br}$	$a^yA^se^{br}e^{br}$
	9	10	11	12
a^yE^m	$A^sa^yE^mE^m$	$A^sa^ye^{br}E^m$	$a^ya^yE^mE^m$	$a^ya^ye^{br}E^m$
	13	14	15	16
a^ye^{br}	$A^sa^yE^me^{br}$	$A^sa^ye^{br}e^{br}$	$a^ya^yE^me^{br}$	$a^ya^ye^{br}e^{br}$

\# 16 — brindle, no mask

\# 12 and 15 — two brindles with mask

\# 11 — fawn with mask

rest — blacks but only 4:16 are true-breeding, i.e., A^sA^s (#1, 2, 5 and 6)

Figure 1 — Cross between a black dog with two brindle genes and a fawn dam with 2 mask genes

A small number of conscientious breeders and many novices have recently been breeding animals from color combinations not recommended by the Color Code of Ethics. Most often, fawns have been bred to blacks in an attempt to improve the conformation of the black lines, although many other color crosses have been attempted. Of all those made, the black *x* fawn is probably the least objectionable since fawn and black will sort themselves out more easily than most combinations. Indeed, such crosses make good sense genetically in the first generation since, by selecting the best blacks from these crosses, really excellent blacks have been produced that are winning in the show ring. These breeders argue that there is just not enough black stock around that compares favorably with the best fawns they will be in competition with. They may well be correct. If they are, the geneticist would say, by all means breed the black to the excellent fawn and get the black trait on the excellent conformation background of the fawn. *But* (and here's the rub), now inbreed those blacks to get them back to a true breeding black because the first generation of such a cross will be a black with fawn genes ($A^s a^y$). This combination has been shown to lead to "rusty" coated blacks in other breeds, though this has not been shown to be true for Danes. If the mixed blacks are properly inbred, a true breeding black ($A^s A^s$) can be retrieved that will retain the best qualities of its fawn ancestors but with true breeding black color. However, what has happened to all the puppies from these crosses that were sold to novices and breeders who did not understand, or, worse, were not told about the problems likely to arise from the breeding of animals with this mixed heritage? If a breeder is willing to keep or destroy or sell only to knowledgeable breeders the puppies from such breedings, more power to him or her. If these mixed heritage puppies are sold to novices as breeding stock without a careful explanation of the pitfalls of such breeding, this is dishonesty by omission. This is what makes the Color Code of Ethics of the parent club such a valuable document. It serves as a guide for persons who don't want to fall into a trap not of their own design. Remember, the above argument would be greatly complicated if other colors were put into the pot. Remember also that this black x fawn argument holds up only if you accept the notion that there is no black stock that compares with the best fawns. There are some black breeders who would vigorously contest that statement.

The *C* gene series

The four genes found in this gene series act to change the intensity of the red-fawn colors found in many dogs as the result either of the $a^y a^y$ or the ee combination. The four genes found in this series are C (full color), c^{ch} (chinchilla), c^e (extreme dilution) and c^a (albino). The last two genes are rarely found in Danes and will not be discussed here. The white Danes encountered in harlequin breeding are the result of the action of the M or merle gene which will be discussed later. The action of the C gene is to produce fawn color of full intensity and, when present in double dose, produces the darker golden or red fawns and brindles that are favored in the show ring. The minor differences in the intensity of

112

fawns and brindles are probably caused, not by the C series but by modifier genes, the action of which is not well understood. When the chinchilla gene (c^{ch}) is present, it will cause a lightening of the fawn color to produce what many fanciers call a washed out fawn or brindle (Cc^{ch}). The washing out of the coat color can be further enhanced by having the chinchilla gene in double dose ($c^{ch}c^{ch}$), although this extent of color loss is probably not seen very often in the Great Dane. Since there appears to be no clear dominant-recessive relationship between the C and the c^{ch} genes, that is, one dose of c^{ch} can be seen as a partial washing out of the color, the breeding of a washed out fawn or brindle to another with normal coloration should be expected to produce offspring, half of which carry the c^{ch} and are therefore washed out in color. Breeding two washed out fawns or brindles (Cc^{ch}) will produce 1:4 normal coloration, 2:4 washed out and 1:4 very washed out ($c^{ch}c^{ch}$).

Trying to breed the washed out character out of your line may be a problem. If it were a simple case of the genes described above, breeding your washed out fawn to an intensely colored partner and then choosing the intensely colored progeny should produce the desired results in one generation. However, the action of modifier genes has not been considered here. Modifiers are genes we know little about but that must be invoked to try to explain the great variability of colors in fawns and brindles. Let's say we have 2 fawns, one of which is deep red fawn and the other is a medium shade of golden fawn. Both would be perfectly acceptable in the show ring and both are CC. Why the difference? This is usually accounted for by invoking modifiers. These genes presumably cause small changes in the amounts of pigment produced, in this case, by the cells in the hair follicle that put the fawn color in the growing hair shaft. The presence of positive ($+$) modifiers would tend to produce more color; the presence of negative ($-$) modifiers would tend to produce less color. Let's further assume (no one knows for sure) that there are three pairs of modifier genes associated with the production of the fawn color. The presence of six positive modifiers ($CC++++++$) would produce a very dark red fawn. The presence of six negative modifiers ($CC------$) would produce a light washed out fawn (like Cc^{ch}) especially if the washed out fawn has a few positive modifiers (say, $Cc^{ch}++----$). You probably couldn't tell unless you did some test breeding. It is fair to say, however, that, to get rid of the washed out color, breed to an otherwise excellent animal which has good color and *has thrown* good color. Keep this idea of modifiers in mind because it will come up again when the harlequin genes are presented. Modifier genes, probably different from those discussed above, may also account for the wide differences seen in the intensity of brindling seen in the ring today, as well as extent of mask and other such variable traits.

The *D* gene series

The easiest way to look at this gene series is as a factor that leads to color dilution wherever dark color is found. This differs from the *C* series in that the *C* series only affects the red-tan colors. The *D* series consists of two genes, *D* and *d*, the *D* being clearly dominant and the *d* recessive. In an otherwise black Dane (A^sA^s or A^sa^y), the presence of the double recessive *dd* will alter the coat color to blue. Since this color is an acceptable one, this is no problem for the breeder of blacks and blues. The *dd* combination can be obtained by breeding blue to blue (*dd* × *dd*), blue to black out of blue breeding (*dd* × *Dd*) or two blacks out of blue breeding (*Dd* × *Dd*). Where the problems show up is when animals are bred where the dilution is not desirable but the dilution is carried as the result of a blue ancestor in the pedigree. Recently a fawn × brindle breeding resulted in two blue fawn and two blue brindle puppies in addition to other normal looking puppies. In such puppies, the fawn areas look quite correct but the black areas of the mask, brindling, leather and nails are blue. On one side of the pedigree, a blue appeared in the 11th generation; on the other side, a blue was found in the 13th or 14th generation. The first blue was called a brindle on the original pedigree but was found to be a falsification on the part of a European breeder. The probability that this dilution could be carried this far without being seen is very small indeed. (Remember, just because a pedigree shows no color problems, this does not say that there weren't odd colors seen in the litters from which the breeding stock came.)

Just imagine how many more problems might be yours if a blue were in the second or third generation, especially if you were either in a line bred or inbred line. This is less likely to be a problem in fawn and brindle lines which tend to be clear of blues, especially in the recent generations. Consider, however, the situation in harlequin breeding. Although many harlequins are bred from harlequin × harlequin breedings, many are also bred from harlequin × black breedings. If the black is from black and blue breeding and if there is blue in the harlequin pedigree, the chances that a *d* will be carried in both partners is a real possibility. This combination could produce a blue harlequin, that is, a harlequin with blue rather than black spots. This is not the commonly seen situation in harlequins where a few merle spots are seen among the black. In the blue harlequin, all spots are blue. This is not an allowable color in the ring in the United States although the color is shown in certain countries in Europe. This is a beautiful color, you say? What do I care what the colors are that I breed? Quite right, providing you don't expect to show your animals and can honestly tell anyone who buys from you that the animal they are buying has color problems and while it may be showable, if you're lucky, it should not be used for a show-breeding program except, possibly, by a very astute and experienced breeder, willing to cull and willing to breed out what are faults, according to our standard. On the other hand, if you want to raise Danes to show and to sell to novice *and* experienced breeders, it is best to avoid the color problems by starting with breeding stock without such problems. You'll have enough other problems more difficult to solve. Colors are easy to trace. A blue harlequin costs as much to raise, to crop and to place as a normal one and cannot demand the price of a properly colored harlequin.

From the discussion above, it must now be clear why there is a distinction made in the GDCA Color Code of Ethics between blacks from black and blue breeding, where the *d* is not a problem, and blacks from harlequin breeding where the *d* is a potential problem. It must also be clear why some harlequin breeders will not permit their studs to be used on a harlequin bitch with a blue in the second, third or even fourth generation. With this in mind, reread the Color Code of Ethics and see what great sense that document makes.

The *G* gene series

This is the greying gene. In dominant form (*GG* or *Gg*), it will cause a black puppy gradually to turn grey as it ages. Such greying occurs routinely in such breeds as the Kerry Blue Terrier and the Poodle. This gene is found in double recessive form (*gg*) in all Danes though very rare appearance of a *G* gene can't be completely excluded.

The *T* gene series

This is the gene which, in dominant form (*TT* or *Tt*), causes the small, dark spots on a light background we call ticking. Generally, ticked animals are born without ticking and the spots gradually form as the puppy grows older. The spots on the Dalmatian are the result of the action of this gene. Dalmatians are born all-white and then acquire their spots as they age. As far as we know, all Danes are *tt*, non-ticked. The rare occurrence of *TT* or *Tt*, however, still must be considered as a possible explanation for the "messy" ones sometimes seen in the ring. In addition, since ticking needs a white or light background to be expressed, an occasional though rare *T* might be present though without detection in self colored Danes.

The *M* gene series

This is the gene that produces a pattern variously called merle or dapple. It produces an animal with variable large areas of grey (merle) and black generally with some white background. This gene may produce a wide variety of expression involving the relative amount of grey and white since the appearance of merles in Danes, Shetland Sheepdogs, Collies and Dachshunds among others is highly variable. Whether this variability is due to the presence of modifiers for the merle pattern is not presently known. To produce the merle pattern, one dose of the dominant form of the gene must be present (*MM* or *Mm*). Since the harlequin pattern in Danes is a modified merle pattern (see the *S* gene series next), all merles and harlequins are *Mm*.

Why not *MM,* you say? Because the *M* gene is what is referred to as a semi-lethal. When present as *Mm*, no problems result. However, when the double dominant (*MM*) is present, the combination, for reason we don't know much about, produces an animal either completely white or white with very small amounts of black. These animals are almost always deaf and/or blind. They are often sterile, though not invariably. Most harlequin breeders cull these animals at birth. Were it not for this semi-lethal condition, these animals would be very valuable in a harlequin breeding program since they could throw nothing but *M*, making all their offspring either merles or harlequins. A prominent harlequin breeder has told me that she had a stud, mostly white with some black spots, which never threw anything but harlequins or merles when bred to harlequin or black. This animal was neither deaf nor blind and was obviously fertile. Presuming that this study continued to perform in this way, this may be an example of a real rarity, that is, a normal *MM* animal. This semi-lethal problem is also seen by breeders of Collies and Shelties.

The *S* gene series

This gene series is sometimes called the spotting gene. It is this series of genes that acts to convert a merle into a harlequin. There are four know genes in this series: *S*—self or completely pigmented coat; *s^i*—Irish spotting, with a few white areas placed as in the Boston terrier in a largely black animal; *s^p*—piebald, that is, large amounts of white, black in large spots or areas; and *s^w*—extreme-white piebald, mostly white with smaller amounts of black in definite areas. In other words, the *S* series, depending on the particular gene pair involved will wipe out the largely grey background of the merle to produce the white background characteristic of the harlequin. The relative amounts of black and white will depend on

116

the combination of *S* genes, with *S* and *s^i* producing more black and less white than *s^p* or *s^w*. Therefore a merle might be *MmSS* or *MmSs^i*. A heavily marked harlequin might be *Mms^is^i* or *Mms^is^p*. A lightly marked harlequin might be *Mms^ws^w* or *Mms^ws^p*. Other combinations are possible to give a variety of patterns. The very wide variety of harlequin patterns suggests that positive and negative modifiers are also at work on the *S* series. If this is true, a harlequin with *s^ps^p* and several negative modifiers might be indistinguishable from an *s^ws^w* harlequin with several positive modifiers.

One of the things that harlequin breeders look for in a "show-marked" harlequin is the presence of a white chest and white front legs, often referred to as a "clean white front." Since the white chest and leg is part of the pattern we call Irish marking (*s^i*), these animals may have at least one dose of the *s^i* gene. At least one harlequin breeder who is knowledgeable about genetics has agreed with this interpretation although there is no real evidence that will stand up in a court of law. If this is true, the ideal show-marked harlequin should be *Mms^i*__ with the blank depending on the relative number of positive and negative modifiers inherited from the parents. If this is true, the harlequin breeders should consider the use of Boston black animals in their breeding programs since the Boston black, black with the clean white front desired by harlequin breeders, is most likely *mms^is^i* or at least *mms^i*__. If the Boston black, although not a color that can be shown in the United States, is an animal with excellent conformation, its genetic contribution can be of real assistance to the harlequin breeder seeking the clean white front. It must be emphasized here, however, that excellence in conformation should be the primary criterion. Some harlequin breeders are willing to sacrifice conformation on the altar of show-color. They certainly have a problem since the acceptable pattern is the only one some judges will put up in the ring, regardless of the excellence in other areas. For this reason, harlequin breeding is a particularly difficult and frustrating experience. When a really good one is produced, however, the extra effort is certainly worth it.

How about another series of questions to round off this chapter? Let's work with the genes of the *A*, *B*, *D*, *E*, *M*, and *S* series only since these are the ones that produce most of the colors. The others (like *C* and *T*) produce only problems, at least for Dane breeders.

9. Write the genetic formula for a Boston marked black.

Ans.: *A^s*__*B*__*D*__*E?E?mms^i*__ Lots of empty spaces but in the absence of breeding information, this is all we can assume.

10. Write the genetic formula for a blue harlequin.

Ans.: *A^s*__*B*__*ddE?E?Mms?s?*

117

11. Write the genetic formula for a fawnikin—a harlequin with fawn spots.

Ans.: $a^y a^y B?B?E?E?E?Mms?s?$

12. Write the genetic formula for two blacks which, when bred, produce a litter containing a blue, a brindle and a fawn both with masks, and three blacks.

Ans.: $A^s a^y B\_\_DdE^m E?mmS?S? \times A^s a^y B\_\_e^{br} E?mmS?S?$

Books to look into for further reading and more information:

1. Almost any high school or college text book has a chapter or two on genetics.

2. Little, Clarence C., The Inheritance of Coat Color In Dogs, Howell Book House, New York, 1957.

3. Burns, M. and M.N. Fraser, Genetics of the Dog, The Basis of Successful Breeding, J.B. Lippincott Company, Philadelphia, 1966.

4. Searles, A.W., The Inheritance of Coat Colour in Mammals, Academic Press, New York, 1969.

Ch. Beacon's Golden Fury V. Geordon, owned by Mr. & Mrs. J. Denio, Jr.

Ch. Temple Dell's Prince Igor, owned by Stephen D. & Elizabeth A. Temple.

11

Nutrition

by J. E. Mosier, D.V.M.

"WE ARE WHAT WE EAT" is a common cliché among those who have a strong interest in nutrition. Individuals involved in the breeding of animals, concerned with maximum health and productivity will paraphrase the statement to "they are what they eat," simultaneously recognizing the impact of genetic selection, environmental factors, general health, and owner contributions.

The production of strong, vigorous, well-formed dogs requires knowledgeable breeder/owners, committed to established goals, who are flexible and adaptable while adhering to basic principles of animal production and behavior.

Feed a Balanced Diet

Good nutrition is dependent on supplying carbohydrate, fat, protein, minerals, vitamins and water to the dog in an appropriate balance consistent with established needs of the dog.

Carbohydrates vary widely in digestibility and must be converted into sugar in the digestive tract before they are available to the dog. While a requirement has not been demonstrated for the dog, carbohydrates do occupy an important role in canine nutrition as a source of energy and in the maintenance of blood glucose levels.

In order to allow for adequate protein, fat, vitamins, and minerals, sixty-seven percent (67%) carbohydrate (dry basis) is said to be the maximum for complete foods. The better quality dog foods contain lesser amounts. Individual animals may not adapt to cereal carbohydrates even when present in relatively lesser amounts.

Problems encountered with carbohydrates other than imbalance of nutrients are usually indicated by diarrhea. Excessive lactose (milk sugar) may tax the capacity of the enzyme lactase and result in diarrhea. Diarrhea induced by feeding milk may be a lactase deficiency. Raw starch in quantity over a period of several days may cause diarrhea. Partly for this reason the processing of commercial dog food includes a cooking process. Diets of high cereal content may result in reduced litter size and reduced viability of puppies.

Proteins are groups of amino acids. Twenty-three (23) amino acids have been identified and ten of the 23 are considered essential. Essential amino acids are those which cannot be synthesized from materials within the animal's body. In certain proteins, one or more of the essential amino acids may be in limited supply, thus the biological value of that particular protein is somewhat limited compared to a protein with balanced amino acid content. Lysine is the primary limiting amino acid in high cereal content diets.

Proteins of muscle, glandular organs, eggs and cheese have a high biological value. Plant proteins rate from good to poor, depending on the source. Proteins from skin, tendons, and gullets are lesser quality than those of muscle and glandular organisms. The protein content of dry food generally ranges from 21% to 25%. The quality of protein may vary considerably depending on the source of protein.

In dry commercial food 60% to 80% of the protein is digestible, while in semi-moist food of the highest quality, the digestible protein may approach 95%.

The quality and quantity of protein is of special importance in gestation, lactation, and during the growth periods of the puppy.

120

Ch. Wallach's Dignity, owned by Dick and Jane Wallach.

Inadequate protein will result in small for birth weight puppies, whelping problems, increased problems with parasitism and coccidiosis, and lustreless hair coats. Evidence accumulates that the inadequate or low protein will affect the temperament and performance of dogs. The production of insulin, thyroxin, and growth hormones is reduced. An inadequate caloric intake can result in the utilization of protein for energy production and will compound the effects of a marginal protein intake.

Dietary fats should supply essential fatty acids, as well as furnishing a concentrated energy source. Fats are essential components of all cells.

Most commercial dry rations contain from 5% to 9% fat. A minimum of 2% of the calories must be in the form of linoleic acid, otherwise a deficiency of essential fatty acids may occur. Fatty acid deficiency is reflected by decreased growth, dry hair, scabby skin, and increased susceptibility to skin infections.

The type of fat in the diet may be significant since the content of linoleic acid is quite variable. Beef fat is notably low in linoleic acid. Plant oils; i.e., corn oil or Wesson oil, are excellent sources.

Improper storage of food may lead to rancid fat. Excessive rancidity can cause loss of hair, loss of appetite, and diarrhea in dogs.

Fats added to foundation diets are an excellent source of energy when dogs are exposed to cold environments or where increased energy demands result from lactation, work, or other forms of stress. Two percent (2%) of the calories must originate from linoleic acid. Increasing the fat content of the ration must consider the energy needs, as well as the potential for induced deficiencies of amino acids resulting from inadequate intake due to the high caloric density of fat-enriched foods.

A variety of minerals are required in the metabolism of the dog. Most commercially-prepared diets contain adequate minerals. Occasionally increased demand, minimal utilization, or poor absorption will lead to deficiency. The need for iron, copper, and cobalt are especially prominent during growth and in the event of blood loss. Other minerals such as potassium, sodium chloride, iodine, manganese, molybdenum, fluorine, sulfur, selenium, magnesium, and zinc fill vital roles in the normal metabolic activity.

Greatest attention is usually focused on calcium and phosphorus and the ratio of one to the other. The ratio of 1.2 parts calcium to 1 part phosphorus is considered optimum. Vitamin D must be present in adequate amounts to assure normal metabolism of calcium and phosphorus.

It is a common practice to supplement the diet with additional calcium or with calcium and phosphorus. Commercial dog foods normally contain adequate amounts of the various minerals, including calcium and phosphorus, to meet the needs of the average healthy adult dog. Growing dogs, pregnant or lactating bitches may benefit by additional quantities of calcium and phosphorus. It is essential, however, that the ratio of calcium to phosphorus be maintained. Excessive calcium may induce a zinc deficiency, especially in pregnant and lactating bitches. Excessive calcium in growing dogs has been incriminated as a cause of abnormal cartilage associated with bone.

The requirement for giant breeds has not been adequately established. Based on observation, it seems appropriate to increase the intake of minerals, especially during gestation, lactation, and periods of rapid growth. Increasing the calcium intake two to three times above the adult maintenance level is a common practice during the growth period. Care must be taken to maintain adequate Vitamin D and proper ratios of calcium to phosphorus. Attention should be given to the potential for induced deficiencies resulting from excessive intake of one or two minerals.

The addition of meat may significantly increase phosphorus intake. Excess phosphorus can interfere with the absorption of calcium and result in abnormal bone. Certain cereals contain phytic acid. Phytic acid may combine with calcium in the digestive tract and convert the calcium into an insoluble form.

As a consequence, one must be selective of any supplemental feeding. This is especially true considering the quantities involved in the feeding of giant breeds.

Vitamins are essential for life. They facilitate many of the body processes involved in normal metabolism. Water soluble vitamins are minimally stored in the animal body, thus the need for constant intake. Fat soluble vitamins; i.e., Vitamins A, D, E, and K, can be stored in sufficient amounts as to negate the need for relatively constant intake.

A deficiency of vitamins is unlikely in normal dogs maintained on quality commercial dog foods. Enteritis, disease, reproduction, rapid growth, heavy work may precede a marginal deficiency. Should the events or signs suggest a need for vitamin supplementation, then the water soluble group can be given without hazard.

Vitamin D holds the greatest potential for adverse effect. Diets should be examined for total Vitamin D content before supplementary quantities are given in order to avoid problems. Excess Vitamin D is most apt to be harmful during the gestation period or during the period of growth. Contrawise, it is during these same periods that inadequate Vitamin D will be most harmful. Thus, the need for careful consideration of recommended allowances during the growth period.

Rickets, or pseudorickets, is a dietary disease of dogs. Bowed legs and enlargement of joints are the most prominent signs; teeth may be irreg-

123

ular and slow to erupt, the signs are a result of Vitamin D deficiency. Simultaneously, a mineral imbalance or deficiency may be contributory.

Vitamin E is common in most foods used in feeding dogs. Long term storage of food under less than optimal conditions may affect the Vitamin E content of dog food. Much of the use of Vitamin E is probably unnecessary. Where a deficiency exists, disturbances of reproduction and lactation have been observed. Increased embryonal death rates and mild deficits in the immune capacity might result.

The use of Vitamin E in breeding bitches has a long history. Current opinion is that well fed dogs probably do not require Vitamin E supplementation. Dogs consuming marginal diets or rancid foods will benefit from the use of Vitamin E. Where Vitamin E is used, one must consider that the vitamin content of wheat germ oil may be adversely affected by long term storage.

The nutritional requirements for the dog are detailed in the National Research Council Bulletin entitled "Nutrient Requirements of the Dog," and in Gaines' "Basic Guide to Canine Nutrition." While the general principles are applicable to all dogs, one must remember that each animal is unique to itself and the requirements might vary according to the health of the digestive tract, the metabolic rate, the work load, and the environmental conditions.

One of the basic functions of nutrition is to provide energy for the biologic system and for the activities of the individual. Energy needs vary with age. Generally the caloric requirement of the puppy is considered to range from 60 to 70 calories per pound of body weight for the first week of life, 70 to 80 calories per pound of body weight the second week of life, 80 to 90 calories per pound of body weight the third week of life, and 100 calories per pound of body weight from the fourth week to weaning. From 85 to 95 calories per pound is highly recommended from weaning until the puppy has reached 40% of its adult weight. From 65 to 75 calories per pound of body weight will generally suffice during the period in which the puppy grows from 40% to 80% of its anticipated adult weight. Fifty (50) to 60 calories per pound of body weight is about average during the period from 80% to 100% of adult weight. The caloric intake required for maintenance of the adult dog will range from 25 to 50 calories per pound.

Given these general averages, the knowledgeable, experienced owner is well aware that the caloric intake must be adjusted according to the individual breed and the individual animal. Many factors, including temperament, activity, digestive ability, biological transport systems, and cellular activity will affect the caloric need. Not all foods have the same digestibility. To be utilized, nutrients must be available to the body cells.

124

Ch. Madas-L of Marydane, owned by Mary K. Johnston.

Quality protein may be 90% to 100% digestible, whereas protein of lesser quality may be 65% digestible.

It is because of these individual factors that the art of feeding must be practiced by the knowledgeable owner. Individual dogs develop certain feeding habits and like different foods, some are nibblers, while others have a tendency to gulp their foods. Some adjust to feeding regimens, others may search for additional food. Some dogs eat competitively while others, less aggressive, may be easily distracted.

As the dog grows older, it is important to adjust the intake to the decreasing metabolic rate. Dogs seven years or older will require 20% to 40% less calories than that suggested for maintenance. Generally speaking, minimum calories at all stages of life except for stress periods will result in a healthier animal with increased likelihood of prolonged, useful life.

The giant breeds are unique to themselves, and unfortunately much of the nutritional information has not been documented by careful research. Such research is essential if the health of the giant breed animals is to be maintained or improved through better nutrition.

In the meantime, we are forced to utilize available information and to strive for better health by pooling experiences and expertise with individual needs and circumstances.

The feeding procedure is usually determined by the owner and by the needs of the individual dog. The choices of free access, limited access, intermittent feeding without pre-set schedules, scheduled feeding time, estimated quantities, weighed quantities provide a wide range of possibilities for both effective and ineffective nutrition.

Selection of feedstuff is usually dependent upon the owner and will be based on personal experience, experience of other owners, or advice of professionals.

Generally speaking, the basic feeding program should consist of a good quality commercial dog food. Those with high cereal content should not be used if maximum nutrition is to be achieved, especially during periods of biological stress.

The feeding program may be influenced by convenience, cost and previous experience. Dry cereal feeds can be fed free choice if the dogs are accustomed to the method. More palatable foods should be fed with due regard to the dog's needs, usually based on weight.

The frequency of feeding is usually based on age. Puppies 1 to 4 weeks of age should be fed 3 to 6 times per day, those 4 to 7 weeks of age should be fed 3 to 5 times a day, puppies 8 to 16 weeks of age should be fed 3 times a day, while those 20 weeks to 18 months of age may be fed 2 times a day. Beyond that time, one daily feeding is adequate. *(Ex-*

perience shows that it is actually better to feed two or even three smaller meals a day to Great Danes,—N.C.D.) Giant breed adult dogs might be better handled by feeding lesser amounts 2 times a day. Once a day feeding may lead to competitive eating and to gulping of feed. In older dogs, smaller amounts more frequently will even the metabolic load on the body.

A variety of factors affect the palatability and intake of food. Fat improves palatability, eliminates sticky or the excessively solid consistency sometimes found in dog foods. Quality protein will enhance palatability. Moistening of dry dog food may increase the intake of calories by 20%. Dogs tend to discriminate against bitter tastes and some dogs become habituated to sweets and certain food. Warm foods are generally preferred to refrigerated foods.

In the housebreaking of dogs, the act of exercising one to two hours after feeding will generally result in bowel action. The movement of food from the stomach into the intestine will stimulate the colon via the gastrocolic reflex.

Problems Related to Nutrition

The breed standard for a given height by six months of age has lead to selection of dogs for rapid growth and large size. Attendant to such a standard are several hazards associated with nutrition.

The problems of osteochondrosis, osteochondritis, hypertrophic osteodystrophy, metabolic bone disease, deviated carpi, wobbler syndrome, and certain conformation problems exemplified by being cow-hocked or splay-footed have both genetic and nutritional bases.

If one accepts the theory that such problems have a nutritional basis, it becomes important that the conclusions be based on documented observations rather than undocumented opinion.

Needless to say, the art of feeding the individual dog rests with the informed owner who is fully cognizant of both the dangers of underfeeding and overfeeding. Discussion between the veterinarian and the owner relative to nutritional status and needs of the dog should occur at periodic intervals. The expertise of the nutritionalist must underlie the nutritional decisions.

Research has demonstrated the results of overfeeding on the giant breed of dogs. Overfeeding of Great Danes has resulted in a variety of bone problems. Hypertrophic osteodystrophy, osteochondrosis dissecans, wobblers, and hip dysplasia are a few of the problems which are triggered or caused by hyperphagia (overfeeding). It seems likely that the problem of hypertrophic osteodystrophy is initiated during the period from weaning to the age of 5 months. While less harm results from overfeeding

127

Left to right: Ch. Danelagh's Saga, Can Ch. Saga's Alataka and Am.-Can. Ch. Saga's Anya.

Am. & Mex. Ch. Tallbrook's Bit O' Honey, owned by S. McCarthy and H. Twaits.

Ch. Kolyer's Rocky Mountain High, owned by Kittie Kolyer.

Kolyer's Kim Tsi, owned by Kittie Kolyer.

after 7 to 8 months of age, one must recognize that overfeeding at any age increases the metabolic load and the impact of limited capacity of the biologic processes on general health. The consequence of hyperphagia is particularly significant when combined with a genetic potential for rapid growth. Affected dogs are lethargic and will watch unaffected puppies play. Splaying of the toes and dropping of the pastern are early signs. Joint enlargement, lameness and pain are especially prevalent in hypertrophic osteodystrophy. In bone dystrophy, one can demonstrate loss of bone density, cortical thinning, and increased density at the zone of provisional calcification by radiographs.

Restricted intake of food so as to maintain growth rate consistent with the published breed growth charts seems particularly effective in the control of hypertrophic osteodystrophy. Severe undernutrition may result in retarded growth and abnormal skeletal structure. Thus, reasonable attention to the caloric intake and growth rate is of special importance in the nutrition of giant breed individuals.

Bloat in association with gastric distention is a dreaded event. While the exact etiology is not well understood, most authorities agree that anatomy, management of feeding and type of feed must be considered. Affected dogs generally eat large quantities of commercial rations.

Feeding in concert with excitement, feeding immediately following hard exercise, and excessive water consumption following feeding all have been associated with the onset of bloat. A variety of opinions have been advanced as to the effect of the character and ingredients of the feed on the incidence of bloat. Oligosaccharide and cereal content have been suspect. Feeding smaller quantities, more frequent feeding, feeding foods of higher caloric density, and the feeding of higher levels of animal protein all have their proponents.

The judicious application of such proposals will lessen the frequency of attacks and may control the incidence almost entirely.

Gestation and Lactation

One will usually note improved performance when the diet of the breeding bitch is supplemented during gestation and lactation. Small quantities of liver, cottage cheese, or hamburger can be added to a commercial dog food without harm. If the supplement is more than 10% of the diet, it is essential that the food be balanced with the recommended ration of calcium and phosphorus. As gestation progresses, the feeding should consist of two divided meals spaced so as to avoid the discomfort of a large, single meal. The quantities fed should be increased starting at the fourth week of gestation. The weekly increase should not exceed

130

10%. During lactation the bitch's feed intake will need to increase dramatically. At the peak of lactation (usually 3 to 4 weeks) the intake may be 2 to 3 times the maintenance level.

Increasing the density of the feed by adding meat and other high fat and protein foods and supplementing the food with Vitamin B complex will help to assure adequate nutritional milk for the puppies. Distressed puppies characterized by mild abdominal distention, softening of the stools, discomfort and crying may respond to the administration of Vitamin B Complex to the bitch. Temperament changes characterized by more aggressive activity on the part of the lactating bitch may respond to the administration of Vitamin C.

Weaning

The weaning of the puppy from the bitch should be a gradual process beginning at 3 or 4 weeks of age.

The initial offering may be homogenized milk plus egg yolk (one egg yolk to one cup of milk). Finely powdered dog food or pablum may be added. If a small amount of milk is put on the puppy's nose, he will lap it off and look for more. Putting the puppy's nose into a shallow pan of the mixture may initiate the feeding mechanism. At 4 weeks of age small amounts of solids may be added. Raw lean meat, ground hard boiled egg, hamburger, canned baby foods are commonly used. At 5 weeks of age a good quality of commercial puppy meal soaked in the milk/egg yolk mixture may be offered. By 6 to 6½ weeks of age the puppy should be eating 4 or 5 meals per day. At that time the puppies can be weaned completely from the bitch. It is also at this time that care should be taken not to push the dogs for maximum growth.

At the time of weaning, the food intake of the bitch should be limited. Total restriction for one day followed by 25% maintenance diet on the second day, 50% maintenance diet on the third day, 75% maintenance diet on the fourth day, and 100% maintenance diet on the fifth day may prevent mammary engorgement.

The puppies are allowed to nurse for 20 minutes two or three times on the first day. The second day they are allowed to nurse for two twenty-minute periods and hand fed the remaining feedings. On day three they are allowed to nurse one twenty-minute feeding and hand fed the remaining feedings. On day four the puppies are hand fed all feedings. While the gradual process of weaning is most popular, there are many methods which can be used with success. Comfort and acceptance on part of the bitch and adequate nutrition on the part of the puppies are the basic tenets of the weaning process.

Coprophagy

Young puppies pass through a period of oral exploration. During that time they may eat their own feces. Older puppies or dogs who eat feces may do so out of boredom and habituation.

Coprophagy may occur on a high carbohydrate diet, when fat is fed to an excess, or where the digestive tract is unable to handle the dietary protein.

Balancing the diet, the use of enzymes, changing the diet, exercise, change of habitat and the use of products to change the odor of the feces may all contribute to the solution.

Management of coprophagy may include avoidance of access to the stool by scheduled exercise or routine pick-up of all excrement.

Flatulence

Dogs in the last one-third of their life span may develop a problem with flatulence. Aging is accompanied by diminished intestinal motility, diminished body activity, decreased cell metabolism, and longer food retention in the intestinal tract which allows longer exposure to the putrefying and fermenting activity of bacteria.

From the nutritional standpoint, certain foodstuff may contribute. Foods with high content of cereal oligosaccharides, certain fatty acids, or excess of meat may contribute to the problem. Confronted with a flatulent dog, one should avoid garbage feeding, high fat diets, excessive meat supplementation, and high soybean content foods. Food sensitivity may be a factor, so that trial feeding of one of the prescription diets such as DD^R, KD^R, or ID^R may be useful. Spreading the food out on a flat pan may reduce gulping and aerophagia. If attempts to control flatulence with nutritional alteration fail, one should consult with his/her veterinarian.

Summary

In summary, the essential step for nutrition of the dog includes:
   I. Provide water—while water is not generally considered a nutrient, the lack of water is a much more serious hazard to health than a lack of food.
   II. Establish a schedule of regularly spaced feeding which is adapted to the living habits of the caretaker and coordinated

Ch. Kolyer's Kaptivating Karlene, owned by Donald & Karlene Pisarick.

Ch. Broadway Annie Oakley, owned by John and Patricia E. Morris.

133

with a program of social training of the dog.

III. Feed a well-balanced diet of good quality and adequate nutrient density. Supplement with care and only with a specific purpose in mind.

IV. Feed for average growth rate, especially during the period from 8 weeks to 7 months of age.

V. If tube feeding is to be utilized, use a 14 or 16 French 18-inch soft tube for the Great Dane puppy.

VI. If calcium is used as a supplement, one must consider the importance for a balanced intake of calcium, phosphorus, and zinc.

VII. The intake of Vitamin D should be calculated and the intake maintained between 9 and 30 units per pound per day.

VIII. Small for birth weight puppies, decreased litter size, congenital abnormalities, decreased immune response, obesity, loss of condition, abnormal stance, digestive upsets, and poor quality hair coat may signify problems of nutrition in a given animal.

IX. The measurement of the nutritional state can be best measured in the adult by red cell count, serum protein, coat quality, conformation, quality of bone and general appearance. In addition, reproductive capability, quality of the parturition, as well as puppy vigor, birth weight and litter size will reflect the state of nutrition.

Ch. Miss Erikke von Riesenhof, owned by David & Eleanor Larsen,

Ch. Von Riesenhof's The Boss, owned by Jim & Jean Fowler.

12

Diseases of the Skeletal System

by J. E. Mosier, D.V.M.

Many of the problems of the skeletal system in the large breed dogs seem to be related to the growth phase. Thus, an understanding of the growth and development of bone is essential to any discussion of the problems.

Flat bones develop as a result of activity of the membrane which covers the surface of bone. This membrane is called periosteum. Periosteum is also responsible for the increase in diameter of the long bones.

Long bones increase in length as a result of activity which occurs between the shaft of the bone (diaphysis) and the ends of the bones (epiphysis).

The area of activity is called the growth plate and is characterized by cartilaginous tissue which progressively converts into bone in the metaphysis and adds to the over all length of the bone.

In periods of rapid growth the area of the growth plate may be quite prominent. The enlargement is a perichondral ring and is frequently referred to as enlarged joints where in reality the enlargement is located a short distance from the joint and around the growth plate.

The conversion to bone involves cells (osteoblasts) which form the organic matrix (osteoid) of primary bone. Primary bone is made porous by action of cells (osteoclasts) which cause resorption and tunnel formation.

Mineralization of the osteoid occurs after a period of maturation. While details of the process of maturation and subsequent calcification are unknown it is known that the process is under control of the osteoblasts. Failure of the osteoblasts to cause maturation of osteoid will result in *osteo malacia.*

Other cells (osteoclast and osteocytes) are involved in bone resorption which if excessive will result in *osteoporosis.*

Osteoporosis constitutes atrophy of bone. While too little bone is present, that which does exist is properly calcified.

Healthy bone involves many factors within the growing dog. Nutritionally, adequate calcium and phosphorous in proper balances and appropriate amounts of Vitamins A, D, C, Copper, Magnesium are required. A variety of hormones including parathyroid hormone, thyrocalcitonin, thyroxin, growth hormone, adrenal cortical steroids, estrogens and androgens are necessary for the development and maintenance of bone.

Mechanical forces and a diversity of other factors like acid base balance, numerous enzymes, citrate, etc. are also involved.

Rickets

Sometimes called rachitis this disease is characterized by failure of adequate deposition of calcium in bones of the growing animal. It is caused by a deficiency of calcium, phosphorus and or Vitamin D. The current availability of commercial foods, Vitamin D enriched milk and food stuffs have resulted in making true rickets an uncommon disease. The National Research Council recommends a daily intake of 240 mg calcium and 200 mg of phosphorus per pound of puppy per day. Properly formulated dog foods have sufficient mineral to meet the needs of young dogs.

Palmer has suggested that Great Dane puppies receive 360 mg calcium and 300 mg of phosphorus per pound of body weight per day during their period of rapid growth. Palmer contends the intake of calcium should relate to the growth rate and cites an increased weight of 100 times the birth weight during the first year in the Great Dane as compared to 60 times for breeds of average size.

High calcium combined with low phosphorus will produce rickets in absence of Vitamin D. It has been demonstrated that low calcium high phosphorus diets would give rise to osteoporosis in addition to rickets.

A deficiency of Vitamin D will result in the production of a cartilage matrix which does not resorb or calcify with the usual dispatch.

The growth cartilage becomes thickened and irregular. The presence of uncalcified cartilage with excess bone matrix will cause enlargement of the area of the growth plate and the cartilage shaft junction (metaphysis). The long bones become soft, may bend and the dog becomes bow legged. Lameness is evident and abnormal eruption of the teeth commonly occurs.

The muscles and tendons seem weak and will result in a pot bellied appearance.

Support of normal weight may cause pain with resulting lameness or disinclination to move.

Treatment of rickets entails the provision of adequate Vitamin D with calcium phosphorus in correct ratio and in appropriate amounts.

Femoral Neck Anteversion

This term is used to describe a change in the angle of the femoral neck in relation to the shaft of the femur.

Affected dogs may show an abnormal gait as a result of instability or subluxation of the hip joint. Hyperextension of the stifle and hock may cause the animal to be post legged. Arthritis resulting from the joint laxity may lead to pain and seeming weakness of the rear quarters.

While the cause of the condition is unknown, it is thought to be congenital in origin. Until such time research reveals the fundamental cause breeders should avoid using affected animals in their breeding program.

Surgery has been employed to correct the defect and to assist in restoration of function.

Retained Cartilage Cores

Hypertrophied enchondral cartilage of the ulna is thought to be related to the rapid growth rate found in the giant breed dog. Severely affected animals will show bowing of the radius and deviation of the carpus due to premature closure of the growth plate. Premature closure will result in shortening or deviation of the affected bone. Similar signs may develop as a result of trauma of the growth plate of the distal ulna. Trauma may also result in partial or complete cessation of growth thus preventing the damaged bone from reaching its predestined length.

Radiographs of apparently normal animals can reveal the presence of a triangular shaped core of cartilage in the distal portion of the ulna. Small cores are often noted in the ulnar metaphyses of clinically normal giant dogs. Retained cartilage cores are thought to be related to over nutrition with accompanying rapid growth. Some authorities advise consideration of genetic cause.

The feeding of a balanced but restricted diet is recommended in order to slow the growth rate.

Where deformity is present corrective surgery can be utilized.

Nutritional secondary hyperparathyroidism

Diets involving excess phosphorus in relation to inadequate calcium will result in hypertrophy or enlargement of the parathyroid glands. The condition is usually observed in animals being fed diets consisting of meat, especially organ meats, and meat by products which alter the ratio of calcium to phosphorus.

A ratio of 1.2:1 (Calcium to phosphorus) is generally recommended.

Low calcium and high phosphorus diets will stimulate the parathyroid gland to produce a hormone which promotes bone resorption, fibrous replacement, and accelerated osteoid formations which fail to become mineralized. Nutritional secondary hyperparathyroidism is most frequently observed in young dogs during periods of rapid growth.

X-rays of the long bones will reveal loss of mineral in the bone along with thinning of the bone cortex. Nutritional secondary hyperparathyroidism is the direct result of the continuous and excessive action of parathyroid hormones on bone. Parathyroid hormone is known to depress osteoblastic activity and to inhibit the mineralization of osteoid. Affected dogs show bowing of the long bones. The bowing is a result of softening with subsequent increased flexibility and deformity. Pathologic fractures of long bones and compression fractures of the vertebrae are some times noted. Immature dogs show varying degrees of lameness and usually exhibit pain when the areas over the growth plates are palpated.

Renal secondary hyperparathyroidism (rubber jaw or renal rickets) will result from chronic kidney disease. The kidneys are unable to excrete phosphate which accumulates in the blood and causes a lowering of serum calcium. In the affected dog the bones of the head will soften and the

Ch. Taboo von Riesenhof, owned by Hazel Gregory.

Ch. Chasnell Sheik of Highfield, owned by Nellie A. Williams.

jaws become rubbery.

Treatment of nutritional secondary hyperparathyroidism consists of carefully planned adjustments in the nutritional program along with limited exercise. Affected animals must be protected from possible trauma until their bones regain normal strength.

Osteochondrosis

This is a disease of cartilage involving a generalized disturbance in the maturation process of cartilage and bone formation. It occurs most commonly during the period of maximum growth rate (4 to 7 months) and in medium to large breed dogs especially males.

In osteochondrosis the articular cartilage becomes abnormally thickened. Small cracks may appear in its surface which will permit the joint fluid to leak through the cartilages and into the underlying bone. Not infrequently a piece of cartilage is undermined so that it forms a flap or partially attached saucer like plaque. The partially attached flap is nourished by the joint fluid and thus may survive for long periods. It is prevented from healing and reattaching to the underlying bone by joint motion and the presence of the joint fluid.

If the piece of cartilage is completely torn loose it may either be reabsorbed or may undergo a process where in it becomes calcified and thus forms a radio opaque joint mouse.

It is important to recognize that osteochondrosis is a generalized condition which affects many different joints of the body. It is the underlying mechanism in retained cartilage in the growth plate of the ulna or radius as well as in osteochondritis of the shoulder, hock and stifle joints.

The importance of trauma as a trigger mechanism is well accepted. However, if it were not for the underlying abnormality of the cartilage trauma would be of little significance.

When the changes associated with osteochondrosis lead to inflammation of the joint the condition is referred to as osteochondritis. When the cartilage flap floats in the joint fluid and inflammatory reaction occurs the term osteochondritis dissecans is applied. The flap or loose body is referred to as a joint mouse. A defect or erosion of the opposing articular surface may result from contact with the loose cartilage.

The primary sign of osteochondritis is a lameness involving one or more limbs which gets worse after exercise. Stiffness is noted after rest. Pain can be elicited by manipulation of the joint. The clinical signs may vary in intensity.

Final diagnosis is based on radiographic examination. Treatment may

140

be medical or surgical depending on the signs and radiographic results. Many cases will respond to conservative approach. Continual lameness beyond a four to six week period should suggest reevaluation and possibly surgery.

Breeders who encounter osteochondrosis will recognize a higher incidence in the offspring of certain dogs. This observation suggests a hereditary predisposition. However, work by Reiland working with pigs revealed that high caloric intake is the primary factor in the etiology of osteochondrosis. Presently it appears that dogs with a genetic capacity for fast growth and "pushed" nutritionally (overfed) during their most active growth period stand the greatest risk of developing osteochondrosis.

The term *Hypertrophic Osteodystrophy* is frequently used to describe one form of osteochondrosis commonly found in giant and large breeds of dogs. The primary clinical signs are acute lameness associated with swelling of the growth plate of the distal radius, ulna and occasionally the tibia.

The affected animal evidences signs of pain when the swollen areas are manipulated. Affected dogs are reluctant to move, may be depressed, refuse to eat and have an elevated body temperature. The acute phase of the disease will last from one to two weeks. Severely affected dogs may have bowing of the radius, premature closure of the growth plate of the ulna, and lateral deviation of the carpus. The swelling of the legs will be most prominent in the area of the growth plate.

Radiographs are useful in demonstrating the extra periosteal calcification.

A variety of treatments have been utilized. Vitamin C, antibiotics, aspirin, corticosteroids all have their proponents. Certain workers have reported little difference in the recovery rate between dogs that have been treated intensively and those that remain untreated. The most effective means of control would appear to be diet restrictions in an attempt to reduce the growth rate. The restrictions should commence at about two months of age and continue till eight months of age. Restrictions beyond eight months will result in slightly decreased height in the dog at maturity. In dogs where the diet is unrestricted beyond eight months of age the genetic potential for height appears to be achieved by time of maturity.

Calcium and Vitamin D should not be used as the treatment since they will generally add to the severity of the condition. Vitamin C is suggested on basis of low levels of Vitamin C found in the urine and blood of affected animals. Large doses of Vitamin C may relieve the pain associated with hypertrophic osteodystrophy. Inadequate Vitamin C may result in subperiosteal hemorrhage as a result of weakness and fragility of the

141

capillaries. When the period of rapid growth ceases the requirement for Vitamin C will decrease significantly. Recent findings indicate that the use of Vitamin C was of no value in some dogs.

Cervical Spondylopathy

This is found in a number of breeds but the Great Dane is most common breed affected. The condition is usually noticed in animals between the ages of eight months and one year.

The condition is thought to have a hereditary base and to involve such factors as rapid growth rate and nutrition.

Affected animals have rear limb uncoordination and a shuffling gait. The toe nails appear worn due to dragging of the feet. Other signs include clumsiness and difficulty in rising from a prone position. The rear legs may cross when forced to walk. Some animals will show atrophy of the shoulder muscles. Diagnosis is dependent on radiographic demonstration of subluxation of the cervical vertebrae, exostosis of the articular facets of the vertebrae and structure of the vertebral canal.

Hip dysplasia

This disease involves a deformity of the hip joint. It is due in part to genetic factors. A number of environmental factors are apparently involved. Rapid growth rate and early maturation appear to be related to the development of hip dysplasia. Other factors which have been incriminated include hormone imbalance, lack of adequate pelvis muscle support and excessive supplementation.

Genetically susceptible dogs forced to grow at a slower pace by controlling their food intake will have a significantly lower incidence of hip dysplasia than dogs fed unrestricted amounts of food. High caloric diets cause overweight, rapid growth, and more severe hip dysplasia.

Osteochondrosis has been incriminated as one of the causes of hip dysplasia. The severity and frequency of both hip dysplasia and osteochondrosis are increased by rapid growth and overnutrition.

Affected dogs may have an abnormal gait and stance. The pelvis will appear higher and flattened dorsally. The stifle and hock joints may appear to be more extended than normal.

Intermittent lameness, loose gait, difficulty in rising will occur to a variable degree. Pain may cause the dog to be cantankerous and relatively inactive.

Palpation and manipulation of the hind limbs cause pain. The disease

142

is progressive and usually leads to the development of secondary osteoarthritis, malformation of the hip joint, subluxation and luxation.

The diagnosis of hip dysplasia is dependent on palpation and radiographic findings. Careful positioning and interpretation by experienced radiologists are essential to the early diagnosis.

Prevention is dependent on careful selection of breeding stock, controlled food intake, feeding of balanced diets and avoiding slick floors during the developmental stages. In addition, excessive supplementation must be avoided.

Treatment includes pectineus myectomy for alleviation of pain, use of analgesic drugs, mild exercise and keeping the dog slightly underweight.

If the lesions are extensive excision arthroplasty, osteotomy or total hip replacement should be considered.

Eosinophilic Panosteitis

Characterized by intermittent shifting lameness, this is common in many breeds of dogs especially in the German Shepherd. Panosteitis can occur at any time between two months and five years of age. The most common age is between five months and twelve months of age.

The cause is unknown. Infections, hereditary, metabolic diseases, allergies, and immune mediated factors have been suggested.

The onset of the disease is sudden. While the lameness shifts from one leg to another it is very seldom that more then one leg is affected at a time. The lameness varies in duration from several days to several weeks. The episodes recur at irregular and unpredictable intervals.

Pressure applied to the shaft of the affected long bone will cause signs of pain. Each attack may vary in intensity with lameness ranging from mild to severe. Appetite and activity may decrease if the pain is severe.

Radiographs of the affected limbs will reveal characteristic densities in the medullary cavity. As the disease progresses proliferation of the periosteum causes thickening and increased density of the cortical bone.

Anti-inflammatory drugs along with pain relievers are sometimes used but do not generally alter the course of the disease.

Tumors: A variety of tumors are found in bone of the dog. The great majority (80%) are *osteo sarcomas*. The remainder are a host of other tumor types including fibro sarcomas, hemangiosarcomas, fibromas, giant-cell tumors.

The most commonly affected bone in the Great Dane breed is the radius. Most bone tumors in the dog are malignant. Diagnosis is based on radiographs and results of biopsy.

143

Treatment involves one or more of the following: immunotherapy, surgery, radiation therapy and chemotherapy. Long term therapy may be required after removal of the primary tumor.

Joint disease of the dog may be divided into non-inflammatory and inflammatory groups. The non-inflammatory group includes *degenerative arthritis* which may be secondary to joint instability such as is found following hip dysplasia or anterior cruciate ligament rupture. Primary degenerative arthritis may follow loss of arterial cartilage associated with aging. Inflammatory arthritis may follow infection, joint hemorrhage or be a result of an immune mediated disease. *Rheumatoid arthritis* is a severe usually progressive arthritis affecting one or more joints. Diagnosis of arthritis is based on history, clinical signs, radiographic evidence, examination of joint fluid and biopsy.

Treatment may involve a variety of therapeutic regimens. Warm dry environment, physiotherapy, anti-inflammatory drugs such as cortisone, surgery, antibiotics, and immuno suppressive agents.

Breeding to minimize the effect of potential genetic factors should be considered when arthritis becomes apparent in a particular line or family.

Selected References

1. Palmer, C. S.; *Osteochondritis Dissecans in Great Danes. Veterinary Medicine/Small Animal Clinician,* October 1979, pp. 994–1002.

2. Olsson, Sten-Erik; *Osteochondrosis—A Growing Problem To Dog Breeders, Gaines Progress,* Summer 1976, pages 1–11.

3. Selcer, R. R., Oliver, J. E.: *Cervical Spondylopathy—Wobbler Syndrome in Dogs, Journal AAHA,* March/April 1975, Vol. 11, pp. 175–179.

4. McKeown, D.; Archilbald, J.: *The Musculo Skeletal System, Canine Medicine 14 ed., Volume 4,* American Veterinary Publication, Santa Barbara, CA, pp. 533–669.

5. Hedhammer, A.; et al.: *Overnutrition and Skeletal Disease: An Experimental Study in Growing Great Dane Dogs, Cornell Vet.* 64 (Suppl. S), 1974.

6. Smith, H.S.; Jones, T.C.; Hunt, R.D.: *The Musculo Skeletal System, Veterinary Pathology,* 4th ed., Lea and Febiger, Philadelphia, PA, pp. 1046–1091.

7. Olsson, S. E.; Reiland, S.: *Nutritional Influence on Osteochondrosis Acta Radiol* (Suppl) Stockholm, 358, 1978, 299.

13

The Dane and Obedience

by Rose Sabetti

THE EARLY NINETEEN-THIRTIES brought something new and exciting to the world and to the sport of dog shows: **Obedience Trials!**

The idea of an obedient and well-trained dog was not new to the world, of course, but the concept of making the training of dogs an adventure of fun, sport and friendly competition to benefit dog and master added a new dimension to the American dog show scene. The Obedience movement was started by Helene Whitehouse Walker, of Carillon Poodles fame, who had witnessed the popularity of Obedience trials in England. On her return to the States she gave all her enthusiasm and her leadership into getting the concept across to fanciers here.

A training class was started in Bedford, New York, with 14 people who began to share her enthusiasm. The well-remembered Blanche Saunders was a trainer and Josef Weber, a former trainer of police dogs in Germany, acted as advisor and teacher. Mr. Weber also taught a class of potential "Obedience Judges," encouraging those who were beginning to show apititude for this part of the work.

The class became incorporated as the Obedience Training Club of New York in 1934. The title of Obedience Training Club of America had been applied for but denied as by this time, another active group had begun work in New England. I was honored to be on the Board of Directors of the Obedience Training Club of New York, and a charter member of the first organized class. I was especially happy to be involved because, as a member of the Great Dane Club of America, I was also representing my favorite breed in this new dimension of the dog world.

Mr. W. Chalmers Burns who later became a member of the American Kennel Club Board of Directors, worked with his harlequin, Bohrer's Bredor at the new Obedience Training Club. My own homebred brindle, Ch. Nero's Anthony, became the first American Great Dane to achieve the twin titles of Companion Dog and Companion Dog Excellent. It will be of interest to those who wonder about Obedience training conducted during show work, to know that Nero won his CD and CDX titles at the same time he was winning groups as well as breed ribbons. This meant he sometimes had to go from the Obedience ring to the show ring on the same day at certain shows. Neither performance suffered.

After the organization of the OTC of NY, classes and clubs were springing up rapidly in numerous places. A training branch of the OTC of NY was started in Port Chester, New York. Shortly after, called the Port Chester Obedience Training Club, it became the major Obedience club and it remains, today, one of the foremost Obedience training clubs in the country.

At this time, all-breed clubs were beginning to include unofficial tests and demonstrations in their shows. Increasing crowds of spectators were to be found around the Obedience rings. The sight of dogs of various breeds and sizes going through their paces, then sitting and lying down together without leashes and waiting for their owners to return to them, never failed to arouse the admiration of the ringside spectators. It was only two years after the first class began that the American Kennel Club, recognizing the public interest in this new aspect of dogdom, held the first licensed Obedience Trial with the North Westchester Kennel Club 1936 show in Mount Kisco, New York.

The titles given by the early Obedience clubs are essentially the same as those now in use. First is the CD, or Companion Dog. Next is the CDX, Companion Dog Excellent, a more advanced stage of the first. Third there is UD, Utility Dog and fourth, TD, Tracking Dog, both more specialized levels of obedience training. A new title of Obedience Champion

146

is now in use.

The famed Westminster Kennel Club held its first Obedience exhibition at its show in Madison Square Garden in 1939. Two teams, all members of the OTC of N.Y., participated and on the ladies team there was a Great Dane, my own Ch. Nero's Anthony. Proudly showing how well he would work with an Irish Terrier, a Dandie Dinmont, a German Shepherd and, of course, French Poodles, he sailed over the jumps (with great dignity) then running around one jump to show the spectators that a Dane could give them a laugh, too. Who says Danes don't have a sense of humor? No melancholy Dane here!

I feel the presence of Great Danes in the Obedience Training Clubs did more to make the Dane popular in the late 1930's and 1940's than any other single cause. People saw that a Dane could be handled by a woman, even a small woman, if properly trained. Suddenly there was evidence that it didn't take sheer strength or a kind of stark training method to make a dog the size of a Great Dane an obedient and pleasant companion.

Many people still ask if the breed takes to Obedience work or whether the individual Danes involved are special dogs with a personal aptitude for such work. That can perhaps best be answered by a look at the participation of Great Danes in Obedience work throughout the United States as reflected in the statistics published by the Great Dane Club of America in their annual yearbooks. Though Danes had won Obedience titles before 1949, such as my own Nero's Anthony, and other pioneer Danes in Obedience work, the Great Dane Club of America first began publishing a list of Obedience titleholders in 1949, officially recognizing the growing presence of the Dane in Obedience work. Such a list of all dogs who have attained one or more of the various Obedience titles has been published every year since.

In 1949, there were 24 Danes listed as having gained one or more Obedience titles. These 24 dogs, though as I stated before there were others who gained their titles earlier, still form a beginning, their presence a symbol of the recognition of the Dane in Obedience work not only by Obedience devotees but by the Great Dane Club of America. They were:

Bradleys King Atlas, W112280, owned by Mr. & Mrs. Elmer A. Bradley
Bradleys Prince von Barkhorn, W119316, owned by Mr. Ray C. Gilmore.
Bruce of Sarne Mere, W26657, owned by Daniel Standish
Cheetah's Beowulf, W73204, owned by William J. Trainor
Dannae of Lestamuir, A944556, owned by Mr. & Mrs. Elmer A. Bradley
Dana of Danedom, W77643, owned by Mr. & Mrs. R. I. Bateman
Don Diego of San Diego, W103976, owned by Mrs. Mardene Zeitvogel

Dux v. Oberhausen, W46449, owned by Catherine E. Miller
Erlandson's Little Girl, W95603, owned by Mr. & Mrs. Peter Hawley
Karry On Kay of Lestamuir, W45301, owned by Thomas W. Tuohy
LeDuc of Closset, W27109, owned by Paul H. J. Hansen
Nel-Hay-Ven Candid Prince, W51435, owned by Von Arnot
Princess Stone Mountain, W104790, owned by Virgil E. Heck
Skipper of Dane Crest, W11038, owned by Rodney H. Davis
Sonny Boy from Berge, W98772, owned by Helen L. Smiley
Trangene's Thumper, W152304, owned by Jeanne Y. and Stanley A. Carlson
The Golden Penny, W77228, owned by Stanley Silberman
Vakeck's Mary Quite Contrary, W24875, owned by Jack and Barbara Riesser
Vakeck's Templar, W50448, owned by John J. Bagley
Boris Laudroadox v. Klausenburg, A923311, owned by Helen M. D'Iorio
Williams' Heide, W31051, owned by Mary V. O'Neill
Lady Cheetah, W11484, owned by William J. Trainor
Birgitta of Stony Hill, owned by Erna M. Funk
Treseder's Fritha, W43183, owned by Florence Treseder

In 1951 these 24 Danes were followed by a listing of 27 Danes gaining their Obedience titles in that year. The year 1954 saw 33 Danes gaining their titles; 1957 saw 39 Danes so honored; 1960 brought 42 Danes achieving their Obedience titles. In 1966, 50 Danes had won titles and in 1969, 66 Danes were listed as Obedience titleholders. Then, in 1971, the Dane in Obedience took a giant leap forward with 150 Danes listed as having achieved their titles. 1975 saw 163 Danes listed, among them one of the most famous of Danes in Obedience ranks, Big Bertha VII owned by Sandy Purdy. Big Bertha, besides her Obedience working titles, was the only Dane to achieve the title of Schutzhund A (a guard or chase dog title) and the Endurance title AD which required a performance of 12.5 miles in two hours.

Of Big Bertha, Sandy Purdy was quoted in an article written by Mrs. Paddy Magnusen as saying that Bertha was no special, unusual Dane at the start of her obedience work. "She was very willing but not too enthusiastic," Sandy Purdy reported, "and Bertha's training began completely by accident. I had purchased her from a teacher at school and did not realize how big Danes get. At four months I started in the Beginner's class at a training school and was quite surprised, as the months passed, how much you can do with a dog. Every waking minute Bertha and I were doing something together (and still are.) Someone suggested I try for a CD title. Naturally, thinking I knew it all, I entered my first show. She busted. I went home and cried and decided never to show again. Bertha and I could just be together and enjoy each other. Little did I realize I was hooked."

From such a beginning came a Dane that has achieved truly unusual heights in Obedience work. Certainly this should be a sign and an encouragement to anyone with a Dane who has wondered about obedience work and whether it takes a special kind of Dane to perform well. Furthermore, the Danes winning titles in obedience work have come from every variety and strain of Dane background, from large kennels, small breeders, championship show stock and pet stock, male and female, famous names and names virtually unknown.

And with this mountain of accumulated evidence on the Dane's ability in obedience, we again become aware that sheer strength is not a necessary ingredient for the handler. So many members of the fair sex have been outstanding in obedience work with Danes. Of the original twenty-four Danes first listed in the Great Dane Club of America yearbook two of the owners mentioned, Erna Funk and Florence Tresedor went on to further involvement in obedience work. Florence Tresedor is still active in the Great Dane world.

So many women have taken part in this phase of the Great Dane world that I couldn't begin to list them all but I do make note here of just a few whom I have observed in the obedience ring and who, I feel, have done exceptional work with Danes in obedience. Among these are Karla Kallahan, Elsie Brennan, Kay Steinfield, Phyllis Bronson, Dee Dee Beck, Eva Robinson (with her famous team), Kathy Krauss, Irene Bourassa and Paddy Magnuson. And none of these women could be termed an amazon.

But whether the Dane can be trained to obedience work is only half the question, the half now more than sufficiently answered. Should a Dane be obedience trained is the other half of the question. My answer is a definite *yes!* This is a giant breed, powerful and heavy, and should always be under control. The basics of obedience training make any breed easier to handle and to live with and with a large breed such as the Dane, I feel it is a necessity. What a joy to have an immediate response to *"down"* when our frisky, gentle giant jumps up on you or your guests. A quick push with the knee or a gentle step on the back toe can make him get down but the command *"down"* can do the job just as well if he or she has been properly trained, and before those loving paws have landed on your shoulders.

It is satisfying to see quick compliance to your "No!" when you see him or her trying to share the *hors-d'oeuvres*, to *"come"* when your curious giant wants to leave the premises. Obedience is learning how words can replace actions and strength for both you and your Dane.

149

The issue of obedience training being incompatible with the show ring is, to my mind, sheer nonsense. I believe that obedience training helps your Dane in his or her show career. True, your Dane will be required during the heeling exercise to sit the moment you stop. However, there is another exercise, the *stand-stay* command where the dog must stand at your side when you stand. It is one of the basic obedience exercises and it can, and should, help your Dane to practice standing for the point-show judge to go over him or her. Obedience training helps your Dane in the show ring in still another way.

We all know of the shy Dane, the "spooky" one. This is the Dane with temperament problems which are sometimes caused by environmental situations and are sometimes the result of hereditary faults. This is the Dane which consistently shies away from the judge.

Obedience training is probably the greatest method of curing this, if it can be cured. Why? First, because the environment of the obedience training ring is different from any other, certainly far different from that of the point show. Climate is an extremely important factor in your Dane's behavior. In obedience class your Dane will be with other dogs having the same problem to one or another degree. In obedience class the trainer must exercise the kind of patience the show ring does not permit. Eventually, in obedience class, your Dane must stand quietly at the end of the leash, then without you holding the leash. He must stand while the judge touches him, pats him and generally goes over him. At the end of this time, your Dane will be far more willing to have the judge in the conformation ring go over him.

There is yet another important aspect of obedience training and your show Dane. It concerns factors which do not concern us enough in our haste to make champions. Dog shows take a tremendous amount out of a dog, physically and emotionally. Anyone who has seen the exhaustion of a dog after a show must recognize this fact. It is a fact which applies to every breed. Certainly the Dane is one to which it applies most strongly. The show ring brings with it a certain tension which your Dane feels. Your Dane feels it in the preparations for the show itself, in the tensions you feel when you start to head for the show.

I am convinced that stress is a factor in many of the health problems to which Danes are particularly subject. I am not in favor of the double-stress of back-to-back shows and today we have more shows planned in clusters of three and four with no rest between. Sometimes it seems we are planning all dog show activities around the easiest way for us or for handlers to amass points rather than what is best for the health and welfare of our dogs. It seems that we too often simply close our eyes to the stress and tensions which our Danes undergo and which, I feel,

150

definitely shorten their life span. There are a few extremely low-keyed, lethargic breeds which the tensions of a show affect less. Even in those breeds, the owners strive for a certain spirit and tension. The Dane is hardly one of those breeds in temperament.

Obedience training can help your Dane cope with the tension of a point show in a much better way. When your Dane is in the obedience classes there is not the tension of the show ring. The atmosphere is relaxed, patient, friendly. It is a far more comfortable and more enjoyable place, this obedience ring, and as, step by step, your Dane absorbs the training routines, a calmer dog develops. This calmer Dane, acclimated to the obedience ring, is far more able to handle the tensions of the point show ring.

I cannot emphasize enough this importance of the climate of the obedience ring where you will find a friendly interest in your dog's work, where those participating enjoy each other's progress and are happy when your dog receives a qualifying score and groan with you when he or she fails in an exercise. In the obedience ring you are judged only by the quality of your dog's and your own performance.

If you have gone to obedience training and turn your dog over to a handler for show ring work, you must inform your handler to use the same commands you have been using in the obedience work. Also, it must be said that not every dog can be properly obedience trained. Sometimes that is the problem of the owner more than of the dog, someone not attuned to the patterns of canine thought processes and behavior. It is not so much a matter of fault but of owners who by temperament are not geared to their dogs. People are all individuals and so are dogs. Some people are not comfortable with certain other people, a condition loosely termed a personality clash. The same general thing happens between some owners and their dogs. In addition, there are some dogs with inherited temperament problems which will defy the range of normal obedience class training procedures. But these are all exceptions to the rule. The usual is that you can train your Dane.

Obedience classes are held now in almost every community. Good books on training are essential but books are only an aid. Weekly attendance at classes, daily practice and patience are the necessary steps in learning how to train your Dane. Do you have to compete or try to earn a title? Not at all. You can pursue obedience training only as far as you wish. Are Danes really good subjects for obedience? They are excellent subjects. As a breed they are quick to respond and certainly intelligent. Physically, a Dane cannot execute the quick responses of the smaller breeds during the normal exercises. It takes longer to tuck those long legs under than it does for a Miniature Poodle. A Dane was never bred for the automatic

151

robot responses so instantly given by the German Shepherds and Dobermans. A Dane, by temperament, tends to think for a moment about what you have said before executing your command. Allowing for individual and breed characteristics, the Dane is an excellent obedience training candidate.

Obedience trials are now 46 years old. Over the years, changes have been made to improve this phase of the sport of dogs. I remember when a dog was required to "Speak on command." I don't recall anyone regretting the change in that rule. However, the basics still remain. A dog is required to heel on and off the lead, come when called, drop on recall, stand and stay singly and in group exercises. In the heel exercise, the dog is required to follow his handler around obstacles. In a trial, this consists of two stewards standing about eight feet apart. The main purpose of this exercise is to teach the dog not to go on the opposite side of people, telephone poles, trees and fire hydrants when you are walking him or her. Anyone who has experienced this with a powerful and exuberant Dane can appreciate the purpose of this particular exercise. There are numerous other exercises, all aimed at practical objectives to help you and your Dane understand each other better.

The Great Dane Club of America awards a trophy to every Dane whose owner is a member of the Parent Club or an affiliate club in good standing, when their dog acquires an obedience title. In 1969, a group of Great Dane enthusiasts formed the Great Dane Obedience Club of California. Still very active, they were of great assistance to the Western Region Committee when holding the Great Dane National Specialty, in 1978. Twenty-seven Danes were entered in the obedience trials. The Midwest Region and the Central Region also provided Obedience Trials with the Great Dane Club of America National Specialty. The Midwest Region, in 1977, had an entry of 24 Danes and the Central Region an entry of 12 in 1979. The January 1981 issue of the *American Kennel Gazette* published the following titles pertaining to Great Danes: 8 Breed Champions; 3 Companion Dogs Excellent; 1 Utility dog and 7 Companion Dogs.

So Obedience and the Dane have both come a long way. The American Kennel Club approves the judges for Obedience trials just as they do those for the breed show ring. Some judges are approved to judge only Novice classes (Companion Dog) while others are qualified for Open, Utility and Tracking classes. If you want to find out about Obedience training classes in your area, the AKC can furnish you with a list of member clubs or all-breed clubs with Obedience classes. An often-quicker way of finding out, and more fun, is to to go a dog show and ask at the Obedience ringside where you'll find lots of people willing to help you get started.

In closing, one last word should be said. Do not take up obedience classes for the wrong reasons. You should go because you want your dog to know you are the master, not to exercise your mastery over the dog. Obedience should not be used as a bolster for your own ego needs. It should be an experience of mutual enjoyment resulting in mutual rewards, not an excursion into the pleasures of discipline. Remember, Obedience should be for the benefit of both you and your dog.

The Great Dane Club of America's Obedience Trophy is a great prize to have on your mantlepiece. The titles C.D., C.D.X., U.D. and U.D.T., and now *Obedience Champion,* are all wonderful additions to your Dane's name. But the greatest reward of all is in showing everyone that you have a truly *great* Great Dane and that you are proud to call him or her your Companion.

Ch. Nero's Anthony, CD, CDX, retrieving over
3 ft. jump bar.

Ch. Dinro Sociable Charm, owned by Bruce and Gloria Morey.

Am. & Can. Ch. Heidere's Moon Shot, owned by Earl Neumann.

14

The Responsibilities
of Breeding

Breeding your great dane is one of the fascinations of owning a dog of fine lineage. It is not a venture for everyone but if you are intrigued with the idea, there are certain basics you should know about, think about and be prepared to cope with before you even begin to think about finding a suitable mate for your dog.

This is the age of the small breeder and by that we mean a breeder with perhaps only one dog, certainly not more than three to five. There are major kennels still in existence. Indeed, there will always be but there are not nearly so many large, professional kennels as there were a few decades ago.

The small, individual breeder has certain disadvantages in the business of breeding fine dogs. The small breeder also has certain advantages. Like virtually everything else in this world, it all depends on how you meet both the advantages and the disadvantages.

The individual breeder had the obvious disadvantage of a limited pal-

Left to right: Riverwood's Mannix, Ch. Riverwood's Marco Polo, Riverwood's Der Sieger and Ch. Riverwood's Regal Siegfried.

Ch. The Kahntinental Gentleman, owned by Inga Silver & Van Kahn.

ette from which to paint his or her genetic pictures. You are limited to the single dog or the very few dogs you have on hand. A mistake in choosing the right mating can not easily be corrected. Large kennels have the advantage of more dogs to pair, and more opportunity to correct errors in future pairings. Large kennels have the advantage of experience, plus a physical plant geared for the business of breeding and whelping. These are not unimportant factors. The small breeder, however, has the advantage of usually being able to devote the kind of personal care and attention to a single litter which large kennels can seldom do. The bitch of a small breeder receives an emotional climate which is usually missing in a large kennel and this is of far more importance, particularly to some bitches, than many realize. There are innumerable, under-the-surface psychological factors that rise within the bitch, most of which we are only beginning to understand. Also, every dog, bitch or stud, is different. The individuality of each animal is still not properly recognized in the way we recognize the individuality of humans. Yet it is very much there and the small breeder has usually a better understanding of the individuality of the dogs in his or her home than the large kennels can muster.

But whether you plan to have a large kennel, or be a small breeder, there are certain unique responsibilities you embrace when you decide to mate your dog, stud or bitch. We do not believe in breeding a bitch because "it would be fun to have a litter," or the "let's do it and see what will happen" attitude. Therefore, we address these words in the assumption that you seriously believe that what you breed, be it one litter or many, will produce a result that will maintain or improve the breed. We assume that you have consulted with others knowledgeable in the field of Danes, studied, watched and listened and finally decided that there are good and valid reasons for you to go into the business of breeding your Dane.

In this connection, you should always keep in mind that the breeding of good dogs is not a matter of simple mechanics. There are no certainties. If it were simply a matter of genetic understanding, any professional geneticist could produce perfect dogs. If it were merely a matter of having the money to buy the best studs and the best bitches, then any person of wealth would be able to produce the finest of dogs. And if it were just experience, then a matter of time would make everyone top breeders. If it were only a matter of having a good "eye," then any fine artist could select the right dogs to mate. All of those elements can and do play a part but there is something more, an undefinable sixth sense which some people have more of than others. In reality, the breeding of fine animals may be more of an art than a science. And genetic chance is always present. So, with all that in mind, there are certain practical, material steps you can take to help yourself, your dogs and the results of your breeding.

Let us start with the owner of the bitch. The foundation of any good breeding program, large or small, rests with the bitch. There is that ovarian nesting ground, that inner cradle where so much that affects the puppies will take place. Of course the first factor is the inherent quality of the bitch herself. Many a fine show bitch does not make a good brood bitch and the reverse is equally true. The genetic background, what is loosely called the bloodlines, of your bitch is vitally important. Your responsibility in this area begins when you buy your bitch. When you breed her you are taking on the responsibility of her bloodlines. It is a serious error to think that you can breed a bitch with serious individual faults or with a poor genetic background to a top show stud and expect the stud to magically wipe out all the problems of the bitch. So look to your bitch, first. It can take generations upon generations of careful breeding to selected studs to correct some faults.

But now you have decided on a certain stud and your bitch as a mating. It has been tradition for the bitch to be brought to the stud for a breeding. There is no genetic reason why it must be done this way. There is no reason why the stud sperm will be affected by travel, any more than the bitch's ovulation. Custom and tradition are tenacious and difficult to change and bringing the bitch to the stud has always been the responsibility of the bitch's owner. It may be heretical but in this day of woman's liberation we see no reason why a stud can't be driven to the place of breeding if it is impractical for the bitch to be driven to the stud. It is time that this aspect of breeding responsibility is shared by both concerned parties. Naturally, I make note of the exception where a particular stud will not perform in any but familiar surroundings. This does occur but not that frequently as anyone watching a potent stud will quickly see.

The responsibility of the bitch's owner does make itself felt in the medical area even before the mating takes place. The bitch must be free of disease before she is bred. You must have your veterinary check her thoroughly. All inoculations should be up to date. Tests for every kind of worm should be made for some worms are particularly damaging to puppies. The bitch should be tested for transmittable viral infections, particularly vaginal ones.

The bitch's owner is responsible for presenting the stud's owner with a proper and accurate pedigree and this must include attention to color. Rightly or wrongly, the stud will share in the blame for the litter to follow so as the bitch's owner you are libeling the stud by an improper pedigree. The bitch's owner is, of course, responsible for the stud fee unless there

158

Am. & Can. Ch. Tallbrook's Dapper Dan, owned and bred by Jacqueline White and Kathleen Twaits.

are other agreements made between the parties regarding this. We feel such agreements should always be confirmed in writing. It is not an indication of mistrust to set things down on paper. The best intentioned and most honest people can understand and interpret things differently as well as remember things incorrectly.

But now you have done all that and are about to proceed with the actual breeding. We feel that the bitch's owner should be prepared to muzzle the bitch, or have her muzzled, particularly with a first breeding. We have seen too many instances where "she's never snapped before," resulting in serious injury to stud and handlers. The owner of the bitch, even if inexperienced in actual breeding procedures, should take part if only to reassure the bitch with a familiar face and voice. Once the breeding has taken place, and there is a "tie," the bitch's owner can help to keep the bitch calm and standing quietly for the necessary time.

If you are shipping your bitch via commercial airline, it is your responsibility to see to everything in that respect. Some airlines do not have properly heated cargo areas for dogs. You must make inquiries about this and follow through with those inquiries. If your bitch is very agitated, be prepared to administer tranquilizers (with your vet's approval). Be certain that the bitch will be met at the other end of the trip. Insurance for the bitch is your responsibility, as are airport handling fees, etc. Any boarding arrangements for the bitch should be settled before the bitch is shipped.

When the breeding is over, you now have the responsibility of your four-footed mother. A proper vitamin supplement and pregnant dietary schedule should be on hand, ready to start, as the result of consultation with your veterinary in regard to your *individual* bitch.

In this connection, it will behoove you to consider all these costs *before* you take that first step to choosing a stud. There will be extra examinations, medications, supplemental diet costs before and *after* birth. There can be complications that arise. Sometimes a caesarian becomes necessary. This can cost between one hundred and three hundred dollars. Are you prepared to assume these costs? If you are not, do not breed.

Once the puppies are due you must be equipped with the correct physical conditions: a whelping box if the bitch is to whelp with you; an area capable of being heated properly for puppies; an area capable of being entirely closed off where no one can wander into by accident. A bitch with puppies can undergo an astonishing transformation of disposition. There will be added medications and supplements for the nursing bitch and for the puppies, worming for the newcomers, shots, etc.

The cropping of the puppies is the responsibility of the owner of the bitch. So are any special medical emergencies which may arise in bitch

160

or puppies. The sale of the puppies is the responsibility of the bitch's owner. Often one is left with more unsold puppies than expected and they all eat. A bitch should not even be bred until she is two years of age, no matter how many seasons she has had, and not used for breeding over seven years of age.

There is another responsibility of the bitch owner of particular importance when breeding harlequins, blacks and blues. We feel you must be strong enough and determined enough to cull the mismarks, the merles and the otherwise poor specimens which are quickly and obviously recognizable. It is the responsibility of the owner of the bitch not to add to the overabundance of improperly marked Danes. The breeding of your bitch extends beyond the show ring. It is not responsible breeding to send unfit specimens out into the so-called pet world. Dogs beget dogs, no matter where they are and all the problems and faults inherited are inherited over and over again as they produce in an unsupervised market. Bad temperaments increase, often aided by malnutrition or illness. Sooner or later it will reflect itself. If a bad-dispositioned, high-strung Dane nearly kills a child, that is all the public will hear. They will seldom, if ever, know that the dog should never have been bred or sold, and that it is not representative of a good Dane properly raised and intelligently handled. All one has to do is look at what such incidents have done to some other breeds.

This, then, is perhaps the last but the greatest responsibility of the owner of the bitch, to keep the unfit out of the public marketplace regardless of sentiment or profit. To do this, is to exercise a higher form of love.

Do you own the stud dog? Then you are not without your responsibilities. First is to have your stud checked for any transmittable viruses. If he has been used on a bitch since you last had him checked, another trip to the vet is in order. It is good procedure to have your stud checked after every bitch he breeds.

Be honest with those who come to you for your stud. If he is an experienced stud and you have the parents, you will soon see things no chart on bloodlines and no pedigree will reveal. You may come to realize, for example, that your stud does not seem to throw the wonderful head he has. On various bitches, that head has not come through to any particular extent. If you are aware that the owners of the bitch have come to you especially for that head, it is your responsibility to tell them that the stud has not significantly thrown that quality. You might have another stud who has strongly thrown the kind of head they seek. In any case, honesty is your responsibility in these matters.

If your stud is inexperienced, and you haven't really a line on what

161

characteristics he does throw, you should tell the bitch's people that fact, also. And the stud's pedigree, like that of the bitch, should be honestly represented, particularly with regard to color. We do not favor using a stud before 18 months of age, preferably not until two years. AKC rules prohibit use of a stud over 12 years of age. If your stud is a young and unproven one, it is your responsibility to provide the kind of experienced help in the actual breeding which will assist both stud and bitch. We favor a minimum of three people at every breeding, more for inexperienced studs and/or bitches. It is also the generally accepted practice of the owner of an unproven stud to allow a repeat breeding if no puppies result from the first breeding. This is often standard procedure with proven studs, also.

It is your responsibility to see that your stud does not carry a line of genetic problems, as far as it is reasonably possible to determine this. You owe it to your stud to see that the bitch is properly muzzled if need be. It is your responsibility to determine, by medical analysis, that the stud you offer does possess live sperm and is in fact a potent breeder on a purely medical level at least.

If a bitch is shipped to you to board during the breeding process, the care of the bitch while you have her is your responsibility. Proper quarters should be provided for the bitch. It is also wise to let the bitch gather herself for a day or two after final breeding before shipping her back to her owners. Crating the bitch properly, getting her safely to the airport, is your responsibility at that end of the trip.

As the owner of the stud, you should properly value the name and the physical evidence your stud produces. For this reason you, as the stud owner, may properly ask that any progeny mismarked or improperly colored will be culled out of the litter. This should be put in writing. It is also your responsibility to sign the litter registration papers promptly. Sometimes, particularly with novice breeders, acting out of all good intent, unexpected elements can develop. The bitch may have gotten herself bred without the owners knowing it and the puppies, to an inexperienced eye, may look all right. If possible, try and visit the litter from your stud personally before signing the litter registration papers. If impossible, try to have an experienced friend check the litter out for you.

The stud owner should be completely frank in the matter of temperament and disposition. If you know your stud has a nasty streak and you observe that in the bitch, you should bring out the fact to be included along with all the other factors which will decide the breeding. A responsible stud owner will insist on at least a three-month period to receive and study the bitch's pedigree and to decide, and advise, on the suitability of the stud. A responsible stud owner will not use his or her stud on those

162

bitches whose owners call up at the last minute, offer a fast rundown on the pedigree and insist on instant servicing. You will actually help such bitch owners by refusal. The breeding of good dogs is not done by hasty, on-the-spot decisions. Remember your responsibility is also to the reputation of your stud. There are more than enough imponderables without adding to them.

We have spoken of the responsibilities of both the bitch owner and those of the stud owner and, as a matter of practical considerations, outlined those duties which fall primarily to each. However, no breeding of good dogs should be approached with a limited responsibility attitude. It is of importance to both bitch and stud owners that the best results possible are obtained from any mating. Honesty in all respects should be paramount on both sides. Experience and advice should be always given when asked for by either side. It is a joint venture and should be viewed as such. The results will reflect on both bitch and stud. If they are all that one can expect, congratulations are deserved all around. If they are not, recriminations are never in order, only the knowledge that you have engaged in an endeavour of imponderables.

Ch. Harldane's Kittie K, owned by Robert Wright.

Am., Can. & Bda. Ch. Crestwood's Charlie Harlie, pictured at 6 years old, owned by Don and Marilyn Miller.

15

The Great Dane Club of America

T HE GREAT DANE CLUB OF AMERICA is a member Club of the American Kennel Club. It was founded in 1889 and is incorporated in the State of New York. One of the oldest of all breed clubs, its first Specialty was held on Long Island, N.Y., in 1910. There were 80 Great Danes entered at that Specialty, a remarkable showing for the time. Between then and now, the Club and the breed have steadily continued to grow.

The American Kennel Club registered 644 Great Danes in 1933 and the Westminster Kennel Club show entry was 82 Danes, making the breed the largest working group entry that year, a scant 44 years after the Club was founded. A list of approved judges was published in the Club publication but not made into an official list until 1937.

By 1936 there had been 318 Dane Championships completed. Of these, it is interesting that 118 were bred in Germany. In 1937, the Great Dane Club of America held its first Futurity, an event that is still held every year. An entry of over 200 puppies was present in 1966.

In 1944, the parent club issued its first *Yearbook.* These marvelous volumes give a real history of the breed in pictures, plus a record of show wins and articles of interest to the fancy. That same year, the club revised the standard and published the first "Official Illustrated Standard" with drawings done by Mr. Donald Gauthier. Once again, the Great Dane Club of America was a leader in the world of pure-bred dogs, the Illustrated Standard a first of its kind.

In 1947, the club initiated a student judging program which in 1973 was expanded into a series of National Educational Symposiums on a great variety of subjects of interest to Dane owners and to dog owners in general. Topics of judging, showing and conformation were part of these symposiums but also included were lectures on health, diet, genetics and a wide variety of other subjects. Breed and all-breed clubs supported these Symposiums and they were given in various parts of the country so that as many fanciers as possible might benefit. The Symposiums were another major "first" in which the Great Dane Club of America has led the way for other clubs.

The Great Dane Club of America is headed by a Board of Directors consisting of 15 members, the President, 1st Vice-President, 2nd Vice-President, Corresponding Secretary, Treasurer and 10 other directors. Its membership is made up of people from all states and some foreign countries, plus Honorary Members.

As the breed has grown in America, so has the parent club. In the United States of America there are now 45 affiliated clubs with additional ones requesting affiliation. This is a testimonial to the operation of the parent club and its farseeing attention to the needs of the members as well as to the growth of the breed. The affiliated clubs represent almost every State. They comprise an approximate membership of 1,200 with 450 members also being members of the parent club.

The parent club is responsible for approving Specialty shows and licensed events, producing the *Yearbook,* writing the official Great Dane Standard (though the American Kennel Club must approve any changes made) and running the annual Futurity. It also has been the leading force in organizing and holding the Educational Symposiums and Regional Specialties, having had 4 Regionals, the last one in Dallas, Texas.

The Great Dane Color of Ethics is well known and is also the responsibility of the parent club. As registration of Great Danes with the American Kennel Club is up to 14,330 for the year of 1980, the activities and the responsibilities of both the parent club and all its affiliated clubs show no signs of lessening. Indeed, the future of the breed will be of paramount concern to all those members of the Great Dane Club of America in the

Ch. Heather of Braeside, owned by Karen Basevitz. Her companion is the renowned Dane fancier, Lena Basquette, who has owned, bred and shown many of the great dogs in the breed for many years.

166

Ch. Castile's Carousel, owned by Ronald and Linda Perozzi and Loren and Lynn Brown.

Am. & Can. Ch. Tara's Sir Fredric Freeloader, owned by Marilyn Riggins.

years to come as it has been in the years past.

The following list of local Great Dane clubs includes their presidents and secretaries in 1980. Since club officers may change from year to year, an inquiry directed to an officer of club on the list should request that the inquiry be forwarded to any succeeding officer.

Local Great Dane Clubs

ALABAMA
Heart of Alabama
President—Mrs. Maude Johnson, 2440 Regent Lane, Birmingham, Al. 35226
Secretary—Mrs. Helen Norred, 4305 Cliff Road, Birmingham, Al. 35222

ARIZONA
GDC of Arizona
President—Robert Browder, 6307 E. Cactus Wren Rd., Scottsdale, Az. 85253
Secretary—Donna Street, 4903 W. Vista Ave., Glendale, Az. 85301
GDC Tucson
President—Robert Edison, 7421 E. Montecito, Tucson. Az.
Secretary—Ruth S. Springstead, 5542 East Kelso St., Tucson, Az. 85712

CALIFORNIA
GDC California
President—Arleen Davis, 2642 Buenos Aires Drive, Covina, Ca. 91724
Secretary—Susan McCarthy, 2631 Greenborough Pl., W. Covina, Ca. 91792
GDC Northern California
President—Capt. Craig Kugler, 345 Plum St., Vacaville, Ca. 95688
Secretary—Mary-Lou Kugler, 345 Plum St., Vacaville, Ca. 95688
GDC of San Diego
President—Chuck Heppler, 8264 Wintergardens Blvd., Lakeside, Ca. 92040
Secretary—Mrs. Bette Temple, 6032 Dehesa Rd., El Cajon, Ca. 92021

COLORADO
GDC of Greater Denver

Am. & Can. Ch. Von Raseac's West Wind, owned by John and Donna Bolte.

Ch. Tilpadane Barnaby Neustadt, owned by Tilly Berenson.

President—Judy Phillips, 6352 Kendall, Arvada, Co. 80003
Secretary—Patricia Gascovny, 7825 W. 24 Place, Lakewood, Co.
80215

FLORIDA
GDC of North Florida
President—Michael J. Rosell, 2718 Southside Blvd., Jacksonville,
Fl. 32216
Secretary—Mrs. Mike French, Orangedale Rt., Box 77, Green
Cove Springs, Fl.
GDC of South Florida
President—Linda Gruskin, 4731 North 36th Ct., Hollywood, Fl.
33021
Secretary—Joanne Bray, 25050 S.W. 187th Ave., Homestead, Fl.
33031

GEORGIA
GDC of Mid-South
President—Merry Carol Houchard, 3250 Gees Mill Rd., Conyers,
Ga. 30208
Secretary—Pam Urban, 285 Green Hill Rd., N.E., Atlanta, Ga.
30342

HAWAII
GDC of Hawaii
President—Evelyn Orkney, 1778 Ala Moana #3014, Honolulu, Hi.
96815
Secretary—Nancy Minuth, 1272 Kina St., Kailua, Hi. 96234

ILLINOIS
Lake Shore GDC
President—Chris Glass, 484 Cottage Hill, Elmhurst, Il. 60126
Secretary—Maria Navigato, 1804 W. Locust, Mount Prospect, Il.
60056

INDIANA
Hoosier GDC
President—Fred Meyer, 110 E. 111th St., Indianapolis, In. 46280
Secretary—Marshia Maish, 913 Isabelle Dr., Anderson, In. 46013

IOWA
GDC Des Moines
President—Dan Miller, 2508 Indianola, Des Moines, Iowa 50315
Secretary—Judith Landers, RR #1, Adel, Ia. 50003

KANSAS *(see Missouri)*

Am., Can. & Bda. Ch. Strawser's Justin, owned by Antoinette Buxton.

KENTUCKY

Kentuckiana GDC

President—Fran Schwartz, 1100 Elm Rd., Lake Forest, Il. 60045

Secretary—Vivian Guntermann, 3910 Elmwood, Louisville, Ky. 40207

LOUISIANA

GDC Greater Shreveport

President—Eugene Savell, 808 Flournoy Lucas Rd., Shreveport, La. 71108

Secretary—Nancy Thompson, 296 Atlantic, Shreveport, La. 71105

GDC of Louisiana

President—Thomas Alexander

Secretary—Karen Wolf, 633 Magnolia Woods, Baton Rouge, La. 70808

MARYLAND

GDC of Maryland

President—Robert Griggs, 146 Teal Dr., Pasadena, Md. 21122

Secretary—Lynne Dalrymple, 2506 Albert Rill Rd., Westminster, Md. 21157

MASSACHUSETTS

GDC of New England

President—Ed. Lyons, 32 Parker Rd., Somers, Ct. 06071

Secretary—Moura Neustadt, 10 Delorenzo Drive, Randolph, Ma. 02368

MICHIGAN

GDC of Michigan

President—Les Denesha, 8030 Agnes, Detroit, Mi. 48214

Secretary—Aileen V. Doughty, 15721 Woodside, Livonia, Mi. 48154

MINNESOTA

Heart of Minnesota GDC

President—James Healy, 1970 Burns Ave., Apt. 228, St. Paul, Mn. 55119

Secretary—Mrs. Lani Atkins, 193 Cottonwood Ct., Stillwater, Mn. 55082

MISSOURI

GDC of Greater Kansas City

President—Lynn E. Brown, Locust Hill Ranch, Box 307, Louisburg, Ka. 66053

172

Ch. Sunridge's Lil' Liza Jane, by Mountdania's Timber ex Ch. Troy's Wendy of Hearth Hill, Best in Show Westchester KC 1974, owned by Marcia A. and Jay A. Lawrence.

Ch. Sunridge's Chief Justice, same breeding and owners as Lil' Liza Jane above.

Secretary—Linda Epperson, 6124 Arlington, Raytown, Mo. 64133
GDC of Greater St. Louis
President—Ralph Graff, MD, 7351 Leasdale, St. Louis, Mo. 63130
Secretary—Laurian Singleton, 715 East Monroe, Kirkwood, Mo. 63122

NEBRASKA
Greater Omaha GDC
President—Robert Ludacka, 4724 Merideth Ave., Omaha, Ne. 68104
Secretary—Dee Heye, Box 145, Hooper, Ne. 68031

NEW JERSEY
GDC of Raritan Valley
President—Pamela Pearl, 1 Deercrest Dr., Holmdel, N.J. 07733
Secretary—Joann Pedicini, 42 Three Brooks Rd., Freehold, N.J. 07728

NEW YORK
GDC of Greater Buffalo
President—Barbara Jung, 679 Franklin St., Springville, N. Y. 14141
Secretary—Charlotte DeMena, 8022 Vallance Rd., LeRoy, N. Y. 14482
GDC of Western New York
President—John Rawleigh, 7 Clearbrook Dr., Rochester, N. Y. 14609
Secretary—Roger Ritzman, 98 Irene St., Buffalo, N. Y. 14207

OHIO
Greater Cincinnati GDC
President—Larry Huber, 6934 Dianna Dr., Cincinnati, Oh. 45239
Secretary—Charlotte McCord, 562 Bratner Lane, Cincinnati, Oh. 45244
GDC of Cleveland
President—Bob Garrett, 8019 Gorge-Orphanage Rd., RD #1, Vermillion, Oh. 44089
Secretary—Jean Scanlon, 29117 W. Willowick, Willowick, Oh. 44094
Heart of Ohio GDC
President—Linda Ridder, 3424 Kite Rd., St. Paris, Oh. 43072
Secretary—Mary Lou Adair, 1551 Stone Rd., Xenia, Oh. 45385
Great Dane Club of Toledo
President—Fred Shea, 538 Indian Ridge, Rossford, Oh. 43460

174

Hannibal and Princess, by Chalon.

Bluker, by Sir Edwin Landseer, R.A.

175

Secretary—Gina Jaeblon, 3856 LaPlante, Monclova, Oh. 43542

OREGON

Williamette Valley GDC

President—Charles McDaniel, 12005 S.E. Juniper, Milwaukie, Or. 97222

Secretary—Deborah McVicker, 236 S.W. Tvalatin Loop, West Linn, Or. 97068

PENNSYLVANIA

GDC of Pennsylvania

President—Pat Higgins, 445 Linden Ave., Woodbury Heights, N. J. 08097

Secretary—Rosalie Kelley, 283 Friendship Dr., Paoli, Pa. 19301

GDC of Central Pennsylvania

President—B. J. White, 11520 Cedar Lane, Kingsville, Md. 21087

Secretary—Barbara Spangler, RD 6, Box 193, York, Pa. 17404

GDC of Western Pennsylvania

President—Anthony Hodges, Mellon Bank, Mellon Square, Pittsburg, Pa. 15219

Secretary—Mary Petrucci, Box 28AA RFD #1, Bentleyville, Pa. 15314

TENNESSEE

GDC of Greater Memphis

President—Rick Beaver, 5361 Egypt-Central Rd., Memphis, Tn. 38134

GDC of Nashville

President—Harry Tucker, Rt. 1, Box 182, Burkett Rd., Antioch, Tn. 37013

Secretary—Mrs. Stan Keely, 4316 Franklin Rd., Nashville, Tn. 37204

TEXAS

Alamo GDC

President—John Brooks, 13925 Anchoridge Hill, San Antonio. Tx. 78217

Secretary—Shirley Padalecki, 319 Creswell, San Antonio, Tx. 78220

GDC of Greater Dallas

President—Kathryn Patterson, 3506 Delford, Dallas, Tx. 75228

Secretary—Faye Hinnrichs, 2716 Arbor Cove, Plano, Tx. 75075

GDC of El Paso

President—Judy West, 4710 Turf 4, El Paso, Tx. 79935

Secretary—Mary McCall, 7815 Basswood, El Paso, Tx. 79925

GDC of Greater Houston

President—Marilyn Riggins, P.O. Box 236, Fulshear, Tx. 77441

Secretary—Terri Burrows, 1210 Roper St., Houston, Tx. 77034

VIRGINIA

GDC of Tidewater

President—Barbara Stehlik, 1513 Alanton Dr., Virginia Beach, Va. 23454

Secretary—Dr. John Stehlik, 1513 Alanton Dr., Virginia Beach, Va. 23454

WASHINGTON, DC

GDC of Metro Washington

President—Dr. James C. Campbell, 15708 White Rock Rd., Darnestown, Md. 20760

Secretary—Carol Stewart, 7211 Central Ave., Takoma Park, Md. 20012

WASHINGTON (State)

GDC of Western Washington

President—Tom Lewellen, 13240-42 Ave. N.E., Seattle, Wa. 98125

Secretary—Herbert Reed, 2137 First Ave., Seattle, Wa. 98121

WISCONSIN

GDC of Milwaukee

President—Mike Muller, 1065 Skokie Ridge Rd., Glencoe, Ill. 60022

Secretary—Pat Behling, W220 S7485 Crowbar Rd. Rt. 2, Muskego, Wi. 53150

16

The Dane In Art

THE DOG has been a part of the history of mankind from the earliest records of human existence. Moreover, dogs have played a close and important role in their relation to man. It is only natural, then, that the history of art, from the earliest of cave and wall drawings, reflects this alliance of dog and man in every aspect of human life.

Therefore, it is an error to speak simply of "dog art." This is a category of art which grew more specialized in the years following the close of the 18th century. Until then, the dog was depicted in art more as a part of the entire painting or wall frieze rather than as a specialized object. The dog was shown more as an integral part of the life and the scenes of that life. The dog was seldom drawn, engraved or even painted alone but in relation to other aspects of life translated into art.

A prime but seldom recognized example of this fact is that even western artists, great masters best known for their religious works, have included dogs in those paintings. Titian, Bassano, Veronese, Botticelli, to name a few, depicted dogs regularly in their most religious works. In Titian's *Last Supper* a dog chews on a bone under the table. Dogs appear in his

The Blue Dane, by Maud Earl.

Pewter Dane, German, sculptor unknown.

The Adoration of the Magi, The Archangel Gabriel with Tobias and many other of his pious works. Veronese had a dog somewhere in almost all of his religious paintings including the *Crucifixion*. The other Veronese, Bonifazio, had a dog in his *Holy Family*, and in his *Deves and Lazarus* he has a dog licking the beggar's sores. Bassano in his *Christ and the Money-Lenders* included a dog, and Raphael drew a large hound in his *The Labours of Adam and Eve*.

The Spanish painters Murillo, de Vargas, Goya and the great Velasquez, whose works were almost a visual history of the kind of dogs in favor during that period, included dogs in many of their works. The Dutch and Flemish painters, Franz Hals, Pieter de Hooch, Van Leyden, Van Eyck, Tenier and the great Rubens constantly painted dogs into their works. Lucas Cranach, Dürer and Hans Holbein were only a few of the great German masters who regularly made the dog a part of their canvases.

The list of English painters who favored dogs in their works would comprise volumes. Chief among them would have to be Hogarth, Sir Joshua Reynolds, Gainsborough, Sir Edwin Landseer and F.S. Turner. It can be said that the era of English artists becoming prominent in the art world also brought more paintings of dogs simply as dogs. But until then, the dog was painted as a part of the scene depicted.

What kinds of dogs did all these and the other artists of history depict and how did the great Dane fare in their works? Actually, taking the entire span of art down the ages, the Dane has fared very well, particularly for a breed of a size which precluded rampant popularity, and whose definition as the breed we know today is barely a hundred years old. Therefore most depictions of the Dane, in the breed's earliest form, are to be found in those works mentioned before where the dog was painted or sculpted not as an object itself but as a part of the entire scene. When newer breeds of dogs began to appear in art, their appearance reflected the changing social conditions and the civilizations of the world.

But long before artists became individually famous for their personal techniques and works, when artists painted wall friezes, carved in stone, worked on monuments and fashioned the decorations for vases of clay, silver and gold, the early Dane was the most frequently depicted dog. By the early Dane we refer to those progenitors of the Danes of today. On ancient Egyptian wall drawings is clearly shown the existence of a variety of dogs, some with straight ears, other with hound ears, some thin and narrow, others with the structural conformations of the Dane. This early Dane is shown on a number of Egyptian wall drawings, notably as one of four dogs pictured on the lower portion of the Limestone Stele of the XII Dynasty at Antef-as. Votive plaques in terracotta from the Babylonian

180

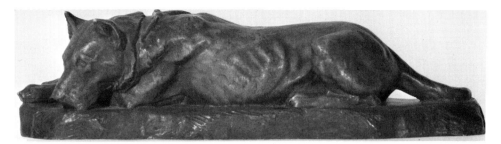

Bronze, by G.L. Guyot.

Bronze, by G. Gardet.

Copenhagen pair of Harlequins, Bing and Grondahl, c. 1850.

era have been found clearly showing the early Dane with hunting collar, and an example of an Egyptian faience status of a puppy is so clearly that of a Dane puppy that no other conclusion can be drawn.

Another piece of evidence of the existence of this early Dane is the tremendous popularity with artists of these early centuries of what has been called the "spotted dog." This "spotted dog" has been found on ancient Sumerian and Babylonian wall drawings, on utensils and artifacts of the early Greeks and Egyptians. To any student of the Dane, this can only be seen as an early example of the breed. Certainly the "spotted dog" of the ancient Greek works is of the anatomical structure, the size and the markings of the harlequin Dane.

One of the most remarkable depictions of the "spotted dog" is an ancient wall painting entitled *The Start of the Boar Hunt* which of itself fits in with the Dane's European history as a hunter of the wild boar. This wall painting, found in the city of Tiryus, Greece, dates back to 1250 B.C. It shows a huntsman holding a huge dog, obviously one of the Greek Molossian hounds and, besides its conformation and size, the harlequin markings are clearly shown. These are true harlequin markings, albeit not quite as harlequins are marked today, yet definitely not the small spots of Dalmatians or other old breeds.

Again, it should be made clear that these old depictions of the early Dane are more than a matter of interpretation because other dogs with definite characteristics were also depicted. Early greyhounds can be recognized, as can early Salukis and certain dogs which, by ear set, stance, shape and general conformation, seem of a breed or type no longer present in any directly recognizable form.

When we go beyond the Greeks and Romans and into the paintings and drawings of European artists of medieval and pre-medieval eras, we again find the early Dane quite distinctly pictured from other dogs shown. We also find they are the most frequently pictured breed. This, too, had its roots in the nature of life itself in those times up through the medieval centuries.

Hunting, then, was not a sport. It was a necessity. Hunting for large game was even more vital. The entire business of the hunt was a matter of earnestness and so art depicting hunting showed the early Danes used in that pursuit. Therefore, the early Danes were seen more than other breeds in the works of the artists of those times as they brought life itself to walls, vases and canvases. During the medieval period, the boar-hunting Dane was drawn again and again by medieval engravers and etchers as they pictured these very important aspects of life.

The early appellation of "boar-hound" given to the Dane going all the way back to the ancient Greeks is again shown most clearly by that same

Miessen porcelain of a Harlequin Dane.

Rosenthal porcelain of Brindle Dane, made for the author.

183

term in a rare print of an obscure artist named Jost Ammon which appears in a German book of various dogs in action, especially in regard to assisting man in the hunt. Printed in 1592, and entitled *Kunstliche Wohlgeriffene neu Figuren von Allerlai Jagt Junst*, it shows the "boar-hound" Danes in the act of bringing down a very large wild boar. Jost Ammon, in this volume, goes on to draw these same dogs individually leaping, running, standing and sitting in particular postures familiar to every Dane owner today.

But when the temper of the times changed, when Europe began to be another society, new breeds appeared and came to the forefront of the shifting social scene. These other breeds began to appear more and more frequently in art. The toy breeds began to show up with regularity in canvases, especially in portraits. Then, as the character of the hunt began to change from one of necessity to one of a gentleman's sport, and indeed the very size and nature of the game changed, the sporting and hound breeds as we know them today began to be the dogs most often depicted in drawings and paintings. Once again, art reflected life. The role of the Dane in art began to decline. The terriers started to become the most popular dog in art as they were becoming in life.

Also, the painting of dogs began to take on the individual nature which it later came to enjoy, and largely still does today. Dogs were drawn and painted of themselves as often as part of a scene picturing humans and events.

However, in the middle 18th century and up through the 19th century, we see the Dane begin to appear again with greater frequency in art. Europe experienced a resurgence of the aristocratic way of life, the spirit of nobility. Strangely enough, this was often at the same time the political climate was swinging the other way. Monarchies may have been in trouble but the great Rhineland Estates in Germany, the Baronial Manor houses of England and the landed Chateau of France were in full flower once again. Perhaps they were a refuge to their inhabitants. The Dane again began to be depicted by major artists on canvas and in sculpture when the breed began to grow in popularity as guardians of the great estates, as the spirit of aristocracy in canine form.

One of the most famous oils of this period is that of *Hannibel and Princess* painted by Henry Barnard Chalon (1771–1849), one of the well known and popular English artists of the time. Sir Edwin Landseer R.A. (1802–1873), though noted for painting one variety of Newfoundland so often that it was named after him, did a pen-and-ink drawing of the Dane *Bluker* in 1819. There was an exhibition of many of his works a few years ago in the Queens Gallery in London as Her Majesty owns several Landseers.

184

.Ch. Danelagh's Fergus, a pastel by Molly Hanford Northrop.

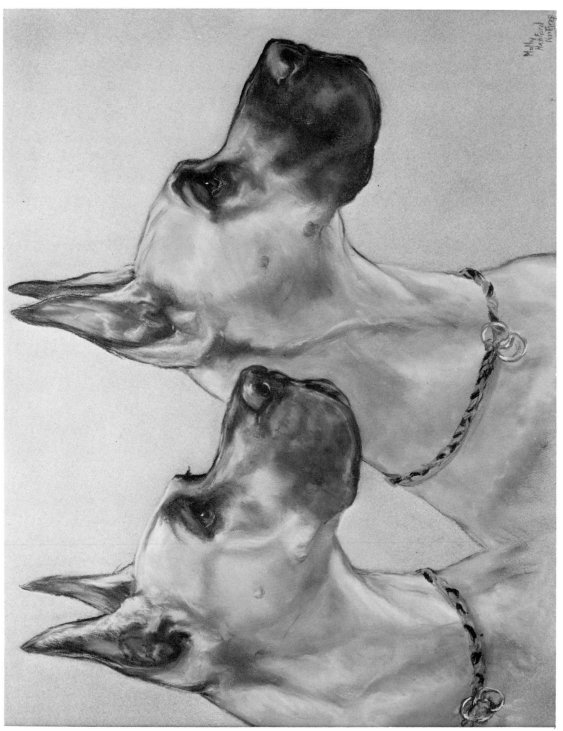

Ch. Danelagh's Jaeger and Ch. Danelagh's Jason, a pastel by Molly Hanford Northrop.

Maud Earl, another well-known British painter who did mostly sporting dogs painted the famous *Blue Dane*. A beautiful rendition of a blue Dane, this is known to be the only Dane painting this great painter ever did. Among other famous Dane renderings in art is that of the great French sculptor, Georges Gardet (1863–1939) who sculpted a dog and a bitch in larger-the-life size bronze in 1880. Only three of these matched pairs are known to exist. Mrs. Marcellus Hartley Dodge, of the days of the famous Morris and Essex Show, owned one of these pairs. Mr. Robert Heal of Canada owns the second pair and where the third set is seems to be a continuing mystery. Gardet did several smaller pieces of the same dog and bitch set which are presumed to be the models for the large pairs. George Lucien Guyot, also a well-known French sculptor, executed a beautiful bronze of a Dane lying down.

In porcelain, the Dane has been well-favored by artists and houses famed in this medium. Meissen, perhaps the most famous name in porcelain, has a lovely harlequin now no longer available. Rosenthal did harlequins and fawns but never a brindle until requested to do so in 1960. In the Danish Copenhagen porcelain there is a blue cast to the black spots on their harlequins but they have done at least six different Danes since the eighteen hundreds. It is most interesting that in an art allied to porcelain, tin-glazed earthenware called faïence in France, Maiolica in Italy and Delft in Holland and England, a most unusual plate contains Great Danes as part of a elaborate border.

This plate was made by the great Maiolica studios of Urbino, the finest craftsmen in Italy in this medium during the 16th century. An example of the *istoriate* style where the subject matter is central to biblical, mythological or narrative scenes, the plate is known as the Leda plate and is part of the collection of the Museo Nazionale del Bargello in Florence. This magnificent plate is bordered by numerous hunting scenes of which one shows two fawn-colored Danes bringing down a black boar and another a fawn and a harlequin combining to bring down a deer. Here, once again, there are other dogs pictured that are definitely not Danes. Again we find the early Danes, in their roles as hunters of large game, to be depicted in still another medium of art.

It is highly unlikely that you will come upon still extant examples of faïence or Maiolica dating back to the 15th, 16th and 17th centuries when this technique of art and craftsmanship reached its full flower. However, if you come upon anything worthwhile in the art field that pictures the Dane, it might be wise to acquire it. Not only could it become a fine investment but it can be the start of a rewarding collection of Dane sculpture and art.

In this regard, old books can be a tremendous source, particularly

15. 10. 1974

A block of stamps and a proof sheet of Congo Republic.

Stamps of Monaco.

genuine, original old volumes. They often contain wonderful old steel engravings or pen-and-ink reproductions that can be a real discovery. The pursuit can have the enjoyment of prospecting for buried treasure with the consequent exciting rewards when one comes up with a real find. Sometimes the prints in old books can be matted and framed to become striking pictures.

The art on postage stamps is another rewarding area for the collector of dog art and Dane art in particular. The tiny Principality of Monaco, famed most for its gambling casinos and Princess Grace, annually features a breed of dog on their stamps issued in connection with their International Canine Exposition. The fawn Great Dane has been so honored. Another country which featured the fawn Dane on its stamps recently was the Sultanate of Oman on the Arabian Sea.

The Congo Republic also issued a series of dog stamps, one of which carried a Great Dane, a blue. Bulgaria, Poland and the German Democratic Republic (East Germany) have all honored the harlequin Dane on their postage stamps and the tiny Republic of San Marino issued a set of dog stamps that included a blue Dane. The United States, with one of the largest dog populations in the world, a nation in which the dog food industry is one of the major industries in dollar volume, has yet to issue any kind of comprehensive canine postage stamp series. We hope that this will one day be corrected and, when it is, that the Great Dane will certainly be among the many breeds so honored.

Not to neglect the present, the dog in art still attracts many contemporary artists and it is hoped that they will make the Dane as much a part of their subject matter as did the artists of the past. Some of the contemporary artists working in the world of the dog will no doubt, in time, achieve the kind of reputation and fame enjoyed by their predecessors. The informed collector should keep a careful watch for the Dane done by contemporary artists. Who knows but that a piece you acquire today may in time become another Gardet or Sir Edwin Landseer. One word of caution, though. Do not suspend artistic judgment or esthetic criteria in a rush to acquire your collection of Dane art. The great pieces of yesteryear are both fine Danes and fine art, representative of their time, place and subject matter on more than one level of excellence.

190

17

Finale-The Great Heritage

ORDINARY BEAUTY is not a constant quality. It tends to change with tastes, social conditions, styles and fashions. Yet there is a beauty which endures, which shines through the changing tastes, the different criteria which different ages bring to the definition of beauty.

The rare illustrations shown here, most of which have never been reproduced before, are more than examples of early German Danes. They stand as a monument to a special kind of beauty, far different than what our modern eye is accustomed to seeing, yet a very real beauty. They are today, seen through the eyes of yesterday.

These pictures are from a book entitled *Die Deutsche Dogge,* printed in Munich in 1887. They are more than a history, more than simply pictures of old Danes. They are an evocation of a time and a spirit, a heritage and a legacy which has been given us to carry on.

Though their dogs were different than ours and their definition of beauty not the same as we see it today, their understanding and appreciation of the Dane is as fitting a description and a criterion today as it was then.

"Power and elegance are united in him in the most wonderful combination. His proud carriage, his high stature, the fine proportions of his limbs, his bright eye, the gloss of his coat, his graceful movements, the harmony of the whole body, makes his intelligence no less remarkable than his fidelity, all these contribute to make him one of the most perfect of animals."

Can any of us today say it better?

»CAESAR«

Besitzer — Propriétaire — Owner: JUL. MAIER, STUTTGART.
Züchter — Eleveur — Breeder: DRESSLER, WANGEN.

I. Pr. STUTTGART 1887.

192

»ELEKTRA«

Besitzer — Propriétaire — Owner: MAX HARTENSTEIN (Zwinger Plavia), PLAUEN i. V.
Züchter — Eleveur — Breeder: BUCHHOLZ, WEISSENSEE.

Ehrenpreis für die beste Dogge aller Classen STUTTGART 1887. — Prix d'honneur STUTTGART 1887. — Cup STUTTGART 1887.

MOREAU

Besitzer – Propriétaire – Owner: K. BLANKENHORN, STUTTGART
Züchter – Eleveur – Breeder: HILLER, OBERESSLINGEN

194

GOLIATH

Besitzer — Propriétaire — Owner: A. SAAGER, STUTTGART.
Züchter — Eleveur — Breeder: HAUSERMANN, STUTTGART.

LEO

Besitzer — Propriétaire — Owner: F. A. ONDERWATER, DUBBELDAM, DORTRECHT.

Ehrenpreis — Prix d'honneur — Cup: HANNOVER 1882, ANTWERPEN 1883, ARNHEIM 1883, LILLE 1883.
I. Pr. ZÜRICH 1881, WIEN 1883, SPAA 1883, MÜNCHEN 1883.

›SULTAN‹

Besitzer — Propriétaire — Owner: E. MESSTER, WESTEND, BERLIN.
Züchter — Eleveur — Breeder: HEUBERGER, STUTTGART.

I. Pr. MÜNCHEN 1879, BERLIN 1880, ELBERFELD 1880.

197

»SANDOR«

Besitzer — Propriétaire — Owner: SCHIEVER, HANNOVER.

II. Pr. BRÜSSEL 1887, I. Pr. ZÜRICH 1887, II. Pr. FRANKFURT 1888, I. Pr. HAMBURG 1888.
Ehrenpreis — Prix d'honneur — Cup: EISLEBEN 1888.

»HUNGARIA NINON«

Besitzer — Propriétaire — Owner: GEZA BUZZI (Zwinger Hungaria), BUDAPEST.
Züchter — Eleveur — Breeder: JUNKERMANN, STUTTGART.

I. Pr. BRÜNN 1887.

NORSEMANN

Besitzer — Propriétaire — Owner: REGINALD HERBERT, CLYTHA, MONMOUTSHIRE
Züchter — Eleveur — Breeder: L. GUHL, HEILBRONN.

I. Pr. LONDON 1887 etc.

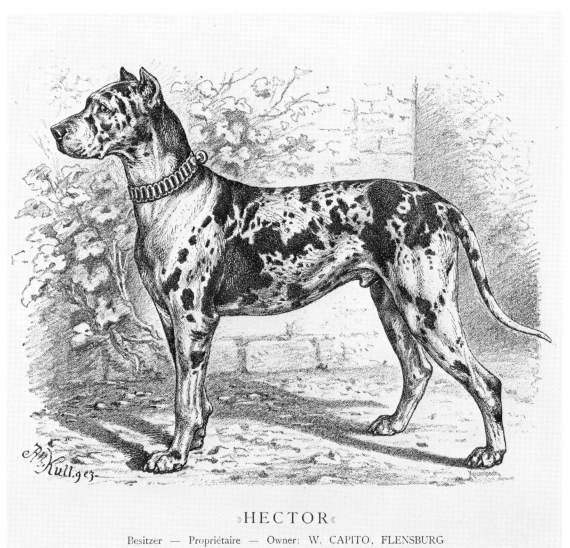

»HECTOR«

Besitzer — Propriétaire — Owner: W. CAPITO, FLENSBURG
Züchter — Eleveur — Breeder: JACOB MAAG, EBINGEN.

Bibliography

1. *Dane Data,* Albert B. Gardner North Hollywood, California, 1936 1st Edition

2. *Diamond Jubilee Yearbook*—Great Dane Club of America, 1961–1963

3. *The New Complete Great Dane*—Howell Book Inc. 1972, 1963

4. *Pure-Bred Dogs*—American Kennel Gazette, American Kennel Club, New York, N. Y. April 1967

5. *Popular Dogs,* Popular Dogs Publishing Co., Philadelphia, Pennsylvania, January 1967

6. *The Complete Great Dane,* by noted authorities, Denlinger 1950

7. *This Is The Great Dane,* by Ernest H. Hart, 1967 T.F.H. Publications, Jersey City, New Jersey

8. Great Dane Club of California, 1931–1963

9. *Last of the Great Scouts*—Helen Cody Wetmore *The Life Story of Colonel William F. Cody,* University of Nebraska Press, Lincoln, Nebraska

10. *Tape Talk* by Rosemarie Robert, *Great Dane Club of America Yearbook,* 1970–1972

11. *The Great Dane Reporter*, Sept./Oct. 1977

12. *Popular Dogs of the Day, No. 14–Great Danes, Dobermanns and Schnauzers*, by Paul C. Blass, 1925

13. *The Great Dane*, by Jean Lanning, 1971

14. *The Origin of the Dog*, Edwin H. Colbert, American Museum of Natural History, Vol. XLIII, N.Y.

15. *The Practical Guide to Dog Breeding*, Eleanor Frankling, Wilfred Funk, N.Y.

16. *The Thinking Dog's Man*, Ted Patrick, Random House, New York

17. *The Dog Owner's Manual*, Josephine Z. Rine, Tudor Publ. Co., New York

LEDA (REG. »LIANE«)

Besitzer — Propriétaire — Owner: J. ZIEBERT, ST. ILGEN, HEIDELBERG

Züchter — Eleveur — Breeder: FR. RIECKERT, HEILBRONN.

II. Pr. FRANKFURT a/M. 1888.